NATURAL RESOURCES

Agriculture

NATURAL RESOURCES

AGRICULTURE
ANIMALS
ENERGY
FORESTS
LANDS
MINERALS
PLANTS
WATER AND ATMOSPHERE

AGRICULTURE

THE FOOD WE GROW AND ANIMALS WE RAISE

Julie Kerr Casper, Ph.D.

CHELSEA HOUSE
PUBLISHERS

An imprint of Infobase Publishing

Agriculture

Chelsea House
An imprint of Infobase Publishing
132 West 31st Street
New York NY 10001

ISBN-10: 0-8160-6352-4
ISBN-13: 978-0-8160-6352-9

Library of Congress Cataloging-in-Publication Data

Casper, Julie Kerr.
   Agriculture : the food we grow and animals we raise / Julie Kerr
Casper.
     p. cm. — (Natural resources)
   Includes bibliographical references and index.
   ISBN 0-8160-6352-4 (hardcover)
   1. Agriculture—United States—Juvenile literature.   I. Title.
S519.C38 2007
   630—dc22   2006027454

Text design by Erik Lindstrom
Cover design by Ben Peterson

Printed in the United States of America

Bang FOF 10 9 8 7 6 5 4 3 2 1

This book is printed on acid-free paper.

CONTENTS

PREFACE
NATURAL RESOURCES:
PRICELESS GIFTS FROM THE EARTH

Mankind did not weave the web of life.
We are but one strand in it. Whatever we
do to the web, we do to ourselves . . .
All things are bound together.

—Chief Seattle

The Earth has been blessed with an abundant supply of natural resources. Natural resources are those elements that exist on the planet for the use and benefit of all living things. Scientists commonly divide them into distinct groups for the purposes of studying them. These groups include agricultural resources, plants, animals, energy sources, landscapes, forests, minerals, and water and atmospheric resources.

One thing we humans have learned is that many of the important resources we have come to depend on are not renewable. *Nonrenewable* means that once a resource is depleted it is gone forever. The fossil fuel that gasoline is produced from is an example of a nonrenewable resource. There is only a finite supply, and once it is used up, that is the end of it.

While living things such as animals are typically considered renewable resources, meaning they can potentially be replenished, animals hunted to extinction become nonrenewable resources. As we know from past evidence, the extinctions of the dinosaurs, the woolly mammoth, and the saber-toothed tiger were complete. Sometimes, extinctions like this may be caused by natural factors, such as climate change, drought, or flood, but many extinctions are caused by the activities of humans.

Overhunting caused the extinction of the passenger pigeon, which was once plentiful throughout North America. The bald eagle was hunted to the brink of extinction before it became a protected species, and African elephants are currently threatened with extinction because they are still being hunted for their ivory tusks. Overhunting is only one potential threat, though. Humans are also responsible for habitat loss. When humans change land use and convert an animal's habitat to a city, this destroys the animal's living space and food sources and promotes its endangerment.

Plants can also be endangered or become extinct. An important issue facing us today is the destruction of the Earth's tropical rain forests. Scientists believe there may be medicinal value in many plant species that have not been discovered yet. Therefore, destroying a plant species could be destroying a medical benefit for the future.

Because of human impact and influence all around the Earth, it is important to understand our natural resources, protect them, use them wisely, and plan for future generations. The environment—land, soil, water, plants, minerals, and animals—is a marvelously complex and dynamic system that often changes in ways too subtle to perceive. Today, we have enlarged our vision of the landscape with which we interact. Farmers manage larger units of land, which makes their job more complex. People travel greater distances more frequently. Even when they stay at home, they experience and affect a larger share of the world through electronic communications and economic activities—and natural resources have made these advancements possible.

The pace of change in our society has accelerated as well. New technologies are always being developed. Many people no longer spend all their time focused in one place or using things in traditional ways. People now move from one place to another and are constantly developing and using new and different resources.

A sustainable society requires a sustainable environment. Because of this, we must think of natural resources in new ways. Today, more than ever, we must dedicate our efforts to conserve the land. We still live in a beautiful, largely natural world, but that world is quickly changing. World population growth and our desire to live comfortably are exerting pressures on our soil, air, water, and other natural resources. As we destroy and fragment natural habitats, we continue to push nonhuman life into ever-smaller pockets. Today, we run the risk of those places becoming isolated islands on a domesticated landscape.

In order to be responsible caretakers of the planet, it is important to realize that we humans have a partnership with the Earth and the other life that shares the planet with us. This series presents a refreshing and informative way to view the Earth's natural resources. *Agriculture: The Food We Grow and Animals We Raise* looks at agricultural resources to see how responsible conservation, such as caring for the soil, will give us continued food to feed growing populations. *Plants: Life From the Earth* examines the multitude of plants that exist and the role they play in biodiversity. The use of plants in medicines and in other products that people use every day is also covered.

In *Animals: Creatures That Roam the Planet*, the series focuses on the diverse species of animals that live on the planet, including the important roles they have played in the advancement of civilization. This book in the series also looks at habitat destruction, exotic species, animals that are considered in danger of extinction, and how people can help to keep the environment intact.

Next, in *Energy: Powering the Past, Present, and Future*, the series explores the Earth's energy resources—such as renewable power from water, ocean energy, solar energy, wind energy, and biofuels; and nonrenewable sources from oil shale, tar sands, and fossil fuels. In addition, the future of energy and high-tech inventions on the horizon are also explored.

In *Lands: Taming the Wilds*, the series addresses the land and how civilizations have been able to tame deserts, mountains, arctic regions, forests, wetlands, and floodplains. The effects that our actions can have on the landscape for years to come are also explored. In *Forests: More Than Just Trees*, the series examines the Earth's forested areas and how unique and important these areas are to medicine, construction, recreation, and commercial products. The effects of deforestation, pest outbreaks, and wildfires—and how these can impact people for generations to come—are also addressed.

In *Minerals: Gifts From the Earth*, the bounty of minerals in the Earth and the discoveries scientists have made about them are examined. Moreover, this book in the series gives an overview of the critical part minerals play in many common activities and how they affect our lives every day.

Finally, in *Water and Atmosphere: The Lifeblood of Natural Systems*, the series looks at water and atmospheric resources to find out just how these resources are the lifeblood of the natural system—from drinking water, food production, and nutrient storage to recreational values. Drought, sea-level rise, soil management, coastal development, the effects of air and water pollution, and deep-sea exploration and what it holds for the future are also explored.

The reader will learn the wisdom of recycling, reducing, and reusing our natural resources, as well as discover many simple things that can be done to protect the environment. Practical approaches such as not leaving the water running while brushing your teeth, turning the lights off when leaving a room, using reusable cloth bags to transport groceries, building a backyard wildlife refuge, planting a tree, forming a carpool, or starting a local neighborhood recycling program are all explored.

Everybody is somebody's neighbor, and shared responsibility is the key to a healthy environment. The cheapest—and most effective—conservation comes from working with nature. This series presents things that people can do for the environment now and the important role we all can play for the future. As a wise Native-American saying goes, "We do not inherit the Earth from our ancestors—we borrow it from our children."

ACKNOWLEDGMENTS

While the fruits of farming are everyone's business, hardly anyone in the United States is in the business of farming today. There is no other country whose people are freer from the toil of having to raise their own food. There is no supply in the world that is more abundant, affordable, or safe than in the United States.

I hope to instill in you, the reader, an understanding and appreciation of farming life. Farmers are our unrecognized heroes. Farming is hard work, and we owe our survival to all the dedicated, hardworking people involved in the production of agriculture. In order to fully appreciate their efforts, it is necessary to understand where food comes from, what it takes to get it to the grocery store, and how much of a bargain it truly is.

I would like to thank the United States Department of Agriculture (USDA); the Agricultural Research Service (ARS); the Cooperative State Research, Education, and Extension Service (CSREES); the Economic Research Service (ERS); and the National Agricultural Statistics Service (NASS) for their constant efforts toward improving the standard of living of the people of the world and for the bounty of information they make available for us to learn from. I would also like to extend special thanks to Debra Spielmaker, coordinator for the Agriculture in the Classroom program based at Utah State University, for her helpful suggestions and guidance during the research for this book.

INTRODUCTION

One of the most important uses of the land's natural resources is for the production of agriculture. We all need to eat, and the cultivation of agriculture affects everyone on Earth. Our connection to agriculture is clear every time we buy a loaf of bread, pick an apple, or eat a slice of pizza.

People all over the world must farm, and certain parts of the world are used for growing certain crops or raising certain animals. For example, tropical locations are needed to grow products like pineapple, sugarcane, and mango. Countries in South America are known for raising beef cattle. America produces vast amounts of wheat and grain. Asia's climate is well suited for producing rice.

America's agricultural production is the envy of the world. The United States has an abundance of fertile soil and good climates in which to grow food. Our farmers and ranchers produce safe, affordable grain for humans; feed grains for animals; meat and dairy products; fruits and vegetables; and fiber crops.

Even with the growth of our cities and the spread of towns and industrial development across the country, the United States is still an agricultural nation. Fifty percent of the country (907 million acres) is cropland, pastureland, and rangeland on privately owned land. This means that the care of half of the United States is in the hands of only 2% of our population. Because of this, it is important that we all understand basic concepts of conservation and land stewardship—the concept that everybody is somebody's neighbor—and that how we care for the land affects much more than we may realize. Even though the private land in America produces an abundance of food, the land also represents many rich, diverse places full of life.

When those places are healthy, they help support the existence of all creatures on Earth.

Farms and ranches in the United States produce much more than food. Well-managed agricultural land also produces healthy soil, clean air and water, wildlife habitats, and beautiful landscapes—all of which are valued by people who live in rural (farming) and urban (city) areas.

A lot of thought, work, and conservation are required for successful agriculture. Healthy, productive land does not just happen. Scientists know farmers can produce abundant food without ruining the Earth. In fact, environmentally friendly farming can help preserve the system that connects humankind with everything else.

Farmers, ranchers, and other landowners have not solved all conservation problems, however. Soil erosion still ruins some land, making it infertile (nonproductive). The continuing growth of towns and cities creates competition for water that was previously used for farming. Agriculture in some areas has hurt biodiversity. The quality of drinking water is also a problem in some areas due to pollution from chemicals used to increase soil fertility in order to grow more crops, or from sediments from soil erosion.

We are very lucky, though, to live in a time of advanced technology. New discoveries and farming techniques continually make agriculture more productive, efficient, and friendly to the environment. Conservation tools that protect the soil and new tools that increase the efficiency of fertilizers, pesticides, herbicides, and irrigation water now exist.

Working with the land in order to protect it—through the use of grassed waterways and riparian (water-related) buffers and by restoring stream channels, for example—has opened up a world of new possibilities for practicing conservation every day.

Agricultural resource concerns are different today than they were 75 years ago in this country, so scientists ask different questions and develop different techniques. We are fortunate to have the benefits of modern technology to guide us. In the future, our grandchildren may ask questions that we have not even thought of; they may use technologies we can only imagine. That is why continued learning of agricultural issues is so important in our complex landscape.

This book about agriculture looks at the development of farming, where the agricultural areas of the world are located, and how agriculture has shaped civilization over time. It reveals how a farm works and how farmers manage to feed the world, why soils and climate are important, and how weeds can be a threat to agriculture. The concept of land stewardship and how everyone shares a part in its success is explored.

Types of renewable and nonrenewable resources are addressed, as well as the concept of sustainable agriculture. Agricultural diversity and alternative farming techniques—such as aquaculture, hydroponics, organic farming, community-based farming, and agroforestry— are presented.

This book explores issues related to why managing the land, water, and soil is a balancing act and why it is so critical; and why recycling, reducing, and reusing are concepts that affect everyone—now and into the future. Finally, it explores the future of agriculture: new technology and developments, synthetic materials, how the U.S. space program is currently playing a role in studies concerning agricultural issues, and how agriculture can be used to create fuel and energy—an exciting concept called *biofuel technology*.

CONCEPTS OF AGRICULTURE

Agriculture is the process of producing food, including grains, fiber, fruits, and vegetables, as well as feed for animals. It also includes raising livestock—domesticated animals such as cows. Besides food for humans and animal feeds, agriculture produces goods, such as flowers, nursery plants, timber, leather, **fertilizers**, fibers (such as cotton and wool), fuels (such as biodiesel), and drugs (such as aspirin, sulfa, and penicillin).

In the Western world, such as in the United States, the use of **genetics** and better **nutrients** have made farming the land much more productive. Our advanced technology has made it possible for fewer people to need to spend time farming. In the third world, where countries are still developing and are not as productive, it is necessary for most people to be farmers because they need to raise or grow their own food.

Modern agriculture depends heavily on engineering and technology. The biological and physical sciences continue to play a critical role and will become even more important in the future, as populations continue to grow and other demands are made on the land. This chapter examines the development of farming, the importance of climate and soil, how a farm works, the struggle with invasive weeds, and the concept of healthy **land stewardship**.

THE EVOLUTION OF FARMING

With the invention of agriculture in about 10,000 B.C., human beings began to take control of their environment. They replaced the natural vegetation with crops so that they could have a dependable food supply in order to survive. Up until that time, people were hunter-gatherers, who had to spend most of their time gathering wild seeds and fruit, and hunting animals. Fortunately, people began to realize that crops could be planted and grown, and animals could be tamed to assist in plowing.

Archaeologists (scientists who study past civilizations) think agriculture may also have started for social reasons—so that people could **harvest** and trade with each other. Whatever the exact reason, there was a gradual transition from a hunter-gatherer lifestyle to an agricultural one, where specific crops were planted at specific times of the year.

Farming began in at least five different places. People in Turkey and the Middle East began cultivating wheat, barley, peas, and lentils. They also began raising sheep and goats. In Southeast Asia, people began to grow vegetables and raise pigs and chickens. In South America, separate agricultural development began in the Andes and the Amazon regions. People living in northern China and West Africa also began their own development of agriculture.

The earliest kind of plow—called an *ard*—that farmers used was crudely constructed of timber, and it just loosened the soil. Early farmers also used digging sticks, the hoe, and the scythe. In addition, they created ingenious systems of irrigation to control water supply. The first significant development, which happened around A.D. 1000, was the moldboard plow. This plow loosened the soil, turned it over, and buried the weeds, leaving the ground ready to plant. Moldboard plows are still used in many parts of the world today and are pulled by animals.

Originally, in about 3500 B.C., oxen (cattle used for pulling equipment) were used to pull primitive plows. Later on, in Europe, the horseshoe and horse collar were invented, and over time, many farmers changed to heavy horses, which could move faster than oxen. Later, in other developing areas, wheels and a seat were eventually added to the plow. Metal parts were then added, which improved the plow's efficiency.

In the western plains of the United States, using the traditional mold-board plow did not work well because it was hard to cut through the dense grass and keep the dirt from sticking to the plow. In 1847, John Deere invented a blade that was "self-polishing" and worked well in the grasslands of the United States. That was how the well-known John Deere Company began. Today, it is a critical part of agriculture and makes high-tech equipment for many aspects of farming.

HOW AGRICULTURE HAS CHANGED CIVILIZATION

When people were living the hunter-gatherer lifestyle, the land could only support a limited number of people. Once crops could be grown, harvested, and stored, all that changed. The advantages of beginning an agricultural society were that a larger population could be supported and the chances of survival were enhanced by being able to store excess food over the winter. Agriculture also allowed people to stay in one place and not have to move around to gather food. It promoted commerce (business and trading) between civilizations, which were able to sell goods and make money. This began the early stages of modernizing the world.

All the major centers of agriculture began along major river systems. Without rivers like the Nile, the Indus, the Huang, the Tigris, and the Euphrates to provide a consistent source of silt (a natural fertilizer) from yearly floods, and water for irrigating crops, agricultural development could not have taken place. It was also during this time that the farmers of the Far East realized they could grow rice on flooded fields.

As farming became more sophisticated, fewer people needed to be farmers. This freed others to pursue scientific, industrial, and cultural paths, which led to many new inventions. This shift made possible developments in architecture, including the building of the huge palaces,

In this photograph taken in 1940, a farmer in Iowa operates a plow and harrow with a team of horses. The use of horses for plowing today is rare in the United States. *(Courtesy of the U.S. Department of Agriculture; photo by John Vachon)*

temples, and theaters for which many famous ancient sites are known. Take, for example, the majestic pyramids of Egypt and the beautiful temples in Greece. Advances in agriculture allowed other people to become scientists and study astronomy, which began the development of navigational skills that were later used to explore the world. None of the major human developments through history would have been possible if agriculture had not been developed. Farming led to a food surplus that could support artists, builders, priests, philosophers, and scientists.

In U.S. history, the sugar mill and Eli Whitney's cotton gin helped to support the system of large plantations based on a single crop. Later, the Industrial Revolution in the late eighteenth century caused the rapid growth of towns and cities and forced agriculture to be isolated within its own area. As inventions like the cultivator, reaper, thresher, and **combine** appeared, modern agriculture further advanced. These advances enabled large-scale agriculture to develop. Modern science also revolutionized food processing, such as with the invention of refrigeration. Today, harvesting operations have been mechanized for almost every plant product. Breeding programs have made livestock production more efficient, too. Genetic engineering has revolutionized growing crops and raising livestock. Agriculture has played a significant role in allowing people to have the lifestyles and freedoms they enjoy today.

DIFFERENT AGRICULTURAL METHODS FOR DIFFERENT ENVIRONMENTS

Farming is not the same all around the world. Because climate, soil, and rainfall vary from region to region, different farming methods work better for different places. In addition, certain areas of the world are better for growing certain types of crops. Some farms are huge, while others are small. Some are operated by large companies, others by individual families. Some farms are modern; others are the same as they were a long, long time ago. No matter what size or type of farm it is, farming is hard work.

In the United States, there are many types of farms, such as dairy farms; grain and cereal farms; ranches that raise **beef cattle**; fruit orchards; cotton, tobacco, and tea plantations; and vegetable farms. The United States is fortunate to have modern equipment, electricity, adequate roads to transport goods, and efficient markets in which to sell goods.

In Asia, rice is an important crop. Farmers may live in small villages next to rice paddies. Many of these farmers use animals, such as water buffalo, to pull their plows, to help with harvesting, and to transport the rice to market. Russia is well known as a producer of wheat. Australia and New Zealand are known for sheep ranching. Sheep are raised for their wool and meat. Ranchers use sheepdogs to herd and keep track of their flocks. A farm in Israel is called a kibbutz. Many people live on the kibbutz and share in the work. Because Israel is hot and dry, these farmers have to terrace the hills, plant trees, dig irrigation canals, and fertilize the soil. These farms are well known today for the large variety of fruits and vegetables that they produce. In Switzerland, where it is very mountainous, farmers raise goats and cows. Many are dairy farmers, whose farms produce milk and cheese. In France, the climate is well suited for growing fruits and vegetables. France is famous for its **fertile** vineyards where grapes are grown, which are later made into wine. In Holland, the farmland lies below sea level. Dutch farmers use pumps and windmills to keep the fertile ground dry enough to farm. Holland is famous for its dairy products, flowers, and vegetables.

In Africa, where there is a tropical climate, farmers grow bananas on huge plantations. The farmers must pick the bananas while they are still green because the bananas must be carried by mule or railroad and then put on boats to be shipped to other lands.

The country of Brazil, in South America, is famous for growing coffee. The farmers there must pick the coffee beans; shell the bean; and then dry, sort, and bag the beans before they can be exported to other places around the world. In Argentina, where there are huge, broad grasslands, the farmers are actually ranchers who raise beef cattle.

No matter what kind of farm a farmer has, he or she must take care of the land. Farmers must keep the soil fertile, irrigate the crops, plant the best seeds, and raise strong animals. The more that technology advances and people learn how to work with the environment instead of against it, the more successful and productive agriculture will be for feeding growing populations.

Agriculture is the science and practice of producing crops and livestock from the natural resources of the Earth. The primary aim of agriculture is to have the land produce abundantly and, at the same time, to protect it from deterioration and misuse. In order to better understand the concept of agriculture, think of the "five Fs": farming, food, fiber, forestry, and flowers.

Farming is the actual production of food and fiber derived from plants and animals. Farmers use many natural resources, such as soil,

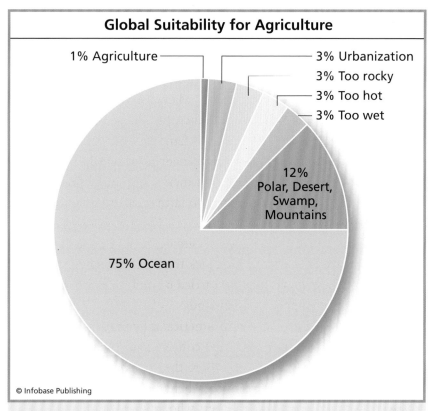

Global Suitability for Agriculture

1% Agriculture — 3% Urbanization

3% Too rocky

3% Too hot

3% Too wet

12% Polar, Desert, Swamp, Mountains

75% Ocean

© Infobase Publishing

This diagram illustrates what the surface of the Earth is used for. Ocean water covers 75%; desert/swamps/mountains/polar regions cover 12%; rocky land with poor soil covers 3%; land areas that are too wet to cultivate cover 3%; land surfaces that are too hot to cultivate cover 3%; land used for urban development is 3%; and land whose soil is suited for agricultural production is about 1%. *(Source: U.S. Department of Agriculture)*

sunshine, water, and air. Farming is a science, but farming is also a business. It is a science because farmers must know about soil, water, weather, chemistry, biology, and **ecosystems**. It is a business because farmers must know about economics, business, and trade.

Food is the product that comes from the farm, such as wheat, oranges, tomatoes, and carrots. The "food industry" involves the processing and distribution of food. *Fiber* includes products like wool or cotton. Wool is the hair of sheep used to make clothing, blankets, and other items, and cotton is a plant product. *Forestry* is the cultivation of trees. Forests provide wood products, paper products, and landscaping products (such as the decorative bark placed under trees in landscaped yards). *Flowers*, also called the "green industry," includes flowers used for indoor decorating, plants for landscaping, and turf (grass sod) for yards.

About one-fifth of Americans are employed in the agricultural industry. The agricultural industry is critical to our survival. It keeps us fed, sheltered, and clothed. It can only continue if humans take good care of the soil, air, water, and other natural resources. Effective **conservation** of the natural resources used in agriculture, as well as good management techniques, must exist so that future generations can enjoy the bounty from the earth as well.

Of the total surface area of the world, most of the land is unsuitable for agriculture. Only 1% of the Earth has soil available for farming. About 75% of the Earth's surface is covered by ocean; 12% is covered with deserts, swamps, mountains, and polar regions; and 12% is too rocky, too wet, too hot, or already being used for buildings.

WHERE THE WORLD'S MAIN FOOD CROPS ARE GROWN

Different parts of the world are suited for producing the various main food crops: wheat, corn, potatoes, rice, barley, millet/sorghum, and starchy roots. Most of the food in the world is grown in the temperate regions—those not too hot or too cold.

Different parts of the United States are better for raising different crops or products. For example, most fresh fruits and vegetables are grown in temperate climates (climates that lack extremes in temperature). States that produce lots of fruits and vegetables are California, Florida, and Texas, not only because of their climates but also because they have longer growing seasons.

The Great Plains (grasslands) grow large amounts of wheat, barley, corn, and other grains. In some of the drier desert areas of the West, where crops cannot be easily grown, ranchers graze cattle and other

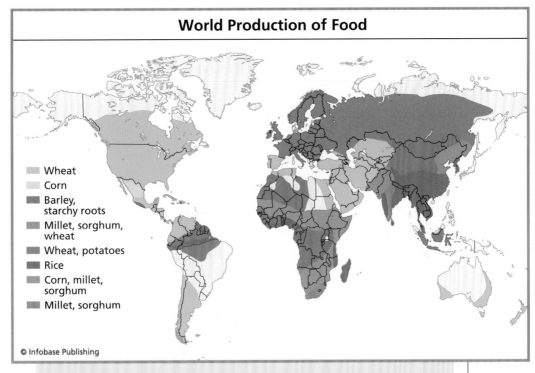

World Production of Food

Wheat
Corn
Barley, starchy roots
Millet, sorghum, wheat
Wheat, potatoes
Rice
Corn, millet, sorghum
Millet, sorghum

© Infobase Publishing

This map illustrates where the world's main food crops are grown. The main food groups include wheat, corn, barley, millet, sorghum, rice, starchy roots, and potatoes. *(Source: U.S. Department of Agriculture)*

livestock. Crops like potatoes grow best in cooler climates, so they are grown in mountainous areas where it stays cooler longer in the spring.

The United States has many types of climates, so many crops can be grown. Because of modern technology for moving, storing, and processing crops, Americans are fortunate to have just about any type of food they want during the year.

FARMING REGIONS OF THE UNITED STATES

For management purposes, the U.S. Department of Agriculture divides the United States into 10 major farm production regions. These regions differ from each other in terms of soil, slope of the land, climate, distance to market, and storage facilities.

The Northeast and the states near the Great Lakes are where most of the country's milk is produced. The climate and soil is good for growing grains that cattle need. The Appalachia region is a major tobacco-producing area. It is also well known for cattle and hog production, dairy farming, and peanuts. The Southeast region is used for raising beef and farming fruit, vegetables, peanuts, citrus fruit, winter vegetables, sugarcane, and cotton.

The Delta region grows soybeans, cotton, rice, corn, and sugarcane. It is also an important area for livestock production. The Corn Belt has an abundance of rich soil and a good climate for farming. This region produces corn, wheat, soybeans, dairy products, cattle, hogs, and feed grains. The Northern and Southern Plains produce the majority of the nation's winter and spring wheat. They also harvest other grains, hay, and cotton and are involved in dairy farming (milk production). The Mountain region is largely used for grazing cattle and sheep. Wheat is also grown there, though, as well as hay, sugar beets, fruits, potatoes, and other vegetables in the irrigated valleys. The Pacific region specializes in wheat, potatoes, fruit, cotton, cattle, and dairy farming. Hawaii is well known for growing pineapples and sugarcane. Alaska has many greenhouse/nursery farms and also produces dairy products.

THE IMPORTANCE OF CLIMATE AND SOIL

Climate and soil are critical to the success of agriculture. No crops will grow when the ground is frozen. They also cannot grow in dry regions where there is no water. Without enough daylight, crops will not grow, either.

Climatic zones are determined by several things, such as latitude and longitude (location on the Earth), elevation, landforms, ocean currents, wind patterns, local and regional weather patterns, and humidity. Areas near the equator are very hot. They also have a lot of rainfall year-round. This is where the tropical rain forests are found. These areas are good producers of rice and bananas.

In areas with a savanna climate—hot and wet summers, and hot and dry winters—more crops can be grown. These areas cultivate sugar-

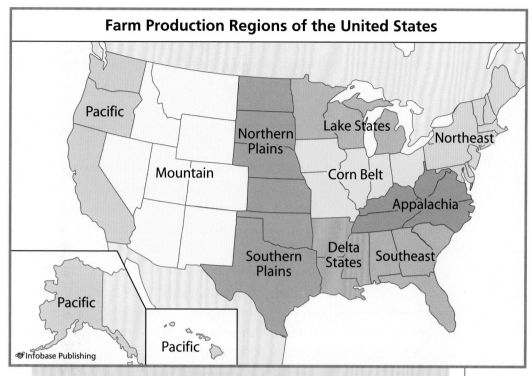

Farm Production Regions of the United States

The ten major farm production regions of the United States. Each region is associated with a specific crop or livestock industry. *(Source: U.S. Department of Agriculture)*

cane, grass, corn, and rice. The desert regions—predominantly hot and dry—are not good areas to grow crops. Providing irrigation is too difficult and expensive. Mediterranean climates, which are dry and hot in the summers, are best for growing bushes and trees that produce olives, figs, and grapes.

Mountain climates also affect what will grow. Areas on the side of the mountain that face the main source of air flow receive more rain than the areas on the other side of the mountain. This is called the *orographic effect*. As an air mass approaches a mountain, the mountain acts like a barrier and forces the air mass upward. As the air rises, it cools, causing moisture to condense into rainfall. This is called the *windward* side of the mountain. As soon as the air mass passes over the mountain, it has little moisture left. The drier air causes a rain shadow effect, or a region of reduced rainfall, on the back (leeward) side of the mountain. Farms on the windward side can be very productive.

Altitude (the height of the land above sea level) is also another climatic factor: the higher the altitude, the cooler the temperature. That is why trees do not grow above a certain level on a mountain. These areas are much too cold to use for agriculture. The effect of climate and weather is critical on a yearly basis, as well. During years of **drought** or too much rainfall, crops can be destroyed. If temperatures drop below freezing, fruit and vegetable crops may be destroyed. When crops get ruined or when there are years of low productivity, this results in food shortages. Food is harder to find and more expensive to buy.

The best farmland in the world is in low-lying areas where rivers have deposited fertile soil and where the climate is moderate. Soil is one of Earth's most valuable resources, because everything that lives on land depends directly or indirectly on the soil. Without soil, farmers could not grow plants, which means they could not grow food for animals or people.

Soil, although it can eventually regenerate, is considered a **nonrenewable resource** because it forms so slowly that it can take hundreds of years for just a few inches (centimeters) to form. A well-developed soil that is extremely fertile could have taken thousands of years to develop. Because of this, farmers must take special care not to harm the soil. If nutrients are removed or the soil is eroded or overused, then crops will not grow well.

Farmers found that, if they did not rotate crops (plant a different type each year), growing the same crop all the time depleted the nutrients in the soil and made the soil infertile (not productive). This happened in the South in the 1800s with the cotton crop. After a few years, cotton would not grow there anymore, and many farmers abandoned their farms. Methods of **soil conservation** had to be put in place to help restore soil fertility.

Soil is much more than just dirt. It contains particles of sand, silt, and clay. These are called inorganic particles. The proportion of these three particles helps determines what type of soil it is. Soil that is high in sand is easy to work with because it has lots of open air spaces between the sand grains, but this makes sand the least fertile soil because the water drains through it quickly, carries away plant nutrients, and leaves the soil dry. Clay soils are more difficult to work with because they tend to be sticky, but they hold more nutrients. Well-drained soils with lots of organic matter are the most fertile soils.

Soil formation is a long, involved process in which soil eventually develops into distinct horizons (horizontal layers). When all the horizons are studied, this is called a soil profile. The surface of the profile is called the **topsoil**. The horizons underneath are called the subsoil, and at the bottom of the profile is bedrock. The soil can either be formed in one place from the weathering of the rock material found in the area, or it can be made from sediments that were first deposited by wind, water, or ice from somewhere else. There are many different types of soil found throughout the world, depending on the rock material they were made from (called parent material).

Soil also has other important components. It must contain water, air pockets, and microorganisms. Tiny organisms live on decaying plants in the soil, turning the plants into **humus**. Humus makes soils more productive because it absorbs heat, holds more moisture, and provides food for growing plants.

Soil formation is also controlled by temperature, climate, and vegetation. Soil is necessary for the production of almost all of our food and fiber. Even crops grown in a water environment—like rice—rely on the nutrients found in soil.

Soil provides 13 of the 16 nutrients needed for plant growth: nitrogen, phosphorus, calcium, sulfur, copper, boron, zinc, manganese, molybdenum, chlorine, iron, magnesium, and potassium. These nutrients come from the weathered minerals and decayed plant matter found in the soil. In addition, carbon, hydrogen, and oxygen are stored in the air spaces between soil particles.

Soil helps filter and **purify** water. When water travels over or through soil before entering rivers or lakes, the soil helps prevent flooding by allowing excess water to soak in for use by plants or to percolate (flow through) to other underground water bodies, called *aquifers*. Soil helps purify contaminated water by removing the impurities and by killing potential disease-causing organisms. Soil is important because it recycles dead plants and animals into the nutrients needed by all living things.

Erosion—by wind or water—is the most serious threat to the health of the soil. This is why soil conservation practices are so important.

HOW A FARM WORKS

How a farm works depends on many conditions. It depends on the type of climate the region has (for example, if a crop needs a warm, moist climate, it will not grow in a dry desert); the length of the growing day (meaning that areas that have more hours of daylight will be used differently than those with a shorter number of daylight hours); the temperature range; the amount of precipitation in the area; the type of soil in the region (for example, crops do not grow well in dry, sandy soil); the size of the farm (if the farm is small, it cannot grow many acres of orchards); the number of employees the farm is able to hire (some crops are more labor-intensive and require more people); and the type of equipment necessary to run the farm (some equipment may be too expensive for a single farmer to buy). These factors will vary based on the type of product produced on the land.

Farmers in developed countries, like the United States, Canada, countries in Western Europe, and Australia, have developed a modern way of farming. Unlike farmers in the past or farmers in developing countries today, most of the jobs once done by hand are now done by machines. The tractor is the most important machine. The farmer uses it to push or pull different kinds of equipment, such as a plow, a harrow for breaking up chunks of earth, or a seed drill for planting.

When hay is grown, a big lawn mover called a *swather* is used. Hay is a staple food for farm animals. Hay is dried alfalfa or dried grass. Alfalfa is usually darker green in color, while grass is a lighter green. When the swather cuts hay, it has a rubber roller inside that crimps the cut stems (squeezes them together). They are crimped so that the stems dry faster. As the farmer drives the swather down the pasture, it leaves a long row of cut hay. The farmer will make several rows in the pasture until all the grass and alfalfa have been cut.

A hay rake is sometimes used if the cut hay needs to be rearranged before a **baler** can be used. This is often used if the hay gets wet before it is baled. The rake fluffs the hay up so it will dry and not grow mildew—which grazing animals do not like.

Balers are machines that scoop up the hay after it has been cut. The baler gathers the hay into bundles by compressing the grass and tying it with a string. Hay bales can be big and round or small and rectangular, depending on the baler used. After the hay is baled, it is moved into a haystack or into a barn for storage using a front-end loader. The front-end loader has a bucket fitted on it with a protruding steel spike. The spike is what lifts the heavy round hay bales (like lifting something with a fork). Once the spike is pushed securely into the bale, the front-end loader tilts the bale so it will not fall off the spike. The bale is then put onto a flatbed truck for transport. Hay is especially important when there is no grass in the pasture during winter. Many farm animals eat hay, including horses, cattle, and elk.

Another important piece of farm equipment is the combine harvester, which can reap, thresh, winnow, and store grain as it cuts a path through a field of wheat. Before the combine harvester was developed, it took the effort of many people to accomplish the same tasks.

Technology is also important for raising livestock. Some animals, like pigs and chickens, are kept in huge farm buildings, where food and temperature can be carefully monitored and controlled. Many types of farm animals are raised in the United States. When farmers raise cattle, they can raise dairy cattle (those used for producing milk and other dairy products) or beef cattle (those raised as a meat supply). Cattle can be fed hay or can graze in a pasture. They eat by moving their heads and tearing the grass in the pasture, because they do not have cutting teeth to bite with. Cattle can also be fed cracked corn. Farmers also put out salt and mineral blocks for the cattle to lick.

Rectangular bales of hay produced from a baler. *(Courtesy of the U.S. Department of Agriculture; photo by Ken Hammond)*

Sheep are another common farm animal. There are about 800 breeds of domesticated sheep in the world. Some sheep are used to produce milk and cheese. Farmers also harvest their wool to make clothes and blankets. Some farmers raise llamas to protect the sheep. A llama is a member of the camelid family, but it does not have humps like its cousin, the camel. Goats are important farm animals all over the world because they can live in mountainous, dry areas where other farm animals (like cows) cannot survive. Goats are often used to produce milk.

The donkey is another common farm animal that has been used for thousands of years. Donkeys can be used for riding, pulling carts, or carrying loads. Mules are also found on farms. A mule is a cross between a female horse and a male donkey. Mules are very strong and sure-footed. Other farm animals include turkeys, ducks, geese, and elk. Dogs and horses are used on farms to help herd animals.

An interesting animal found on some American farms is the beefalo—a cross between the American bison and cattle. The beefalo is a hearty, strong animal. It can tolerate the heat and the cold. The beefalo does not require specific grasses for feed, but instead is able to eat whatever grasses are available. Because these animals are easy to handle and produce rich milk, they make a good farm resource.

Farms produce many types of produce, such as cherries, pears, peaches, apples, oranges, and apricots. Where they are grown depends on the climate, temperature, and growing season. If fruit trees freeze in the spring once the blossoms are out, the fruit crop for that year can be destroyed.

Many types of grain are grown on American farms, such as barley, sorghum, soybeans, rice, and wheat. There are a variety of vegetables grown on farms. Some of the most common are potatoes, carrots, beets, turnips, onions, garlic, lettuce, asparagus, green beans, cabbage, squash, pumpkins, corn, green peas, peppers, and sweet potatoes. In many places across the United States, farmers collect the produce they have grown and sell it at **farmer's markets**, which are very popular because the produce is always fresh.

A combine harvester cultivates a wheat crop. *(Courtesy of the U.S. Department of Agriculture)*

Although modern agriculture is much more efficient and more food can be produced today than ever before, sometimes there are drawbacks. Many farmers use chemicals to improve their produce. They use fertilizers to help crops grow and **herbicides** and **pesticides** to kill weeds and insects that can damage crops.

Some farmers have stopped using chemicals and have switched to **organic farming** and a practice called **crop rotation** (growing different crops each season) to keep pests down instead of using pesticides. They use animal **manure** instead of chemical fertilizers and **herbal** remedies instead of antibiotics.

Another problem with modern farming is that sometimes farmers grow so much grain that they cannot sell it at a profit. Sometimes governments buy it and store it. Governments try to keep the supply and demand balanced so that farmers do not grow too much and lose money or do not grow enough and make food prices rise out of control. It is a challenge to balance food supplies to accommodate surpluses (areas with too much food) and shortages (areas with too little food). Sometimes in developed countries, governments pay farmers a **subsidy** not to produce too much. Other governments have tried fining farmers for producing too much of a **commodity**.

In less-developed, poorer countries, there is a different problem: not enough food to feed the population. **Famine**, starvation, and **malnutrition** are common problems in these countries. Sometimes, other countries will send emergency food supplies to these nations, but this is not a long-term solution. Farmers in these countries need to produce their own food and adopt land conservation practices that allow them to farm more productively. Sometimes the reasons for shortages are financial, but in other instances, farmers just lack the proper education. These issues are covered in more detail in later chapters.

THE THREAT OF INVASIVE PLANTS AND WEEDS

Native plants have evolved over millions of years to fill unique **ecological niches**. Invasive weeds are nonnative (did not originate in the area they are growing in) and ecologically damaging plants.

Invasive weeds are plants that developed in other regions. Growing in their own regions, they are not considered invasive weeds that harm the environment because they developed within the local ecosystem. They are naturally controlled by competition with other plants and by insects, diseases, and other predators. When their population increases in the region they originated in, insects and other predators keep them under control.

The term *weed* is used to describe any plant that is unwanted and grows or spreads aggressively. An invasive plant is a plant that is growing where it should not be. A pineapple in a pumpkin patch would be an example of an invasive plant because it does not belong there, just as an orchid would be in a strawberry patch. Some invasive plants become a problem because they grow aggressively and crowd out native plants.

One of the greatest obstacles scientists and land managers face today in promoting **ecosystem health** is the rapid expansion of invasive plants. Some invasive plants and noxious weeds (which are harmful to human or animal health) can produce significant changes to vegetation, composition, structure, and ecosystem function. These aggressively growing plants destroy farmland and wildlife habitat and can reduce plant diversity (choke out other types of plants).

Weeds know no boundaries. They are invading government-managed public land, farms, forests, parks, and private lands. Millions of

Facts About American Agriculture

- The food and fiber industry accounts for 20% of America's production and employs 20% of our population.
- Agriculture is the United States' biggest employer. More than 21 million people have a job that is related to agriculture and the food industry.
- One farmer can feed 129 people.
- Americans spend roughly $2,328 each year on food for each person.
- In the year 1900, it took 35 to 40 labor hours to produce 100 bushels of corn. Today, only 2.5 hours and 1 acre of land are needed to produce the same amount.
- There are 2.7 million farms in the United States. Women operated 145,156 of those farms.
- In 1994, farmers placed 36.4 million acres of their land in reserve to protect the environment and provide habitat for wildlife. This means that farms and ranches provide habitat for 75% of the nation's wildlife.

Adapted from the Utah Agricultural Applied Technology Program,
http://www.usoe.k12.ut.us/ate/ag/

acres of once healthy, productive rangelands, forested lands, and riparian (river) areas have been overrun by noxious or invasive weeds. Weeds can dominate and cause permanent damage to natural plant communities. Scientists and land managers realize the seriousness of this problem and understand that, if weeds are not controlled, they can damage the health of the land.

This problem is especially pronounced in the western regions of the United States. Because so much ranching and grazing of livestock occurs on private ranches and **public lands** in the West, weeds pose an increased threat to the health of the land there. If weeds are allowed to take over an area and compete with native plants for soil nutrients and space, the native plants will die. Because livestock graze the native plants and depend on these for their food supply, weeds need to be controlled.

The same concept applies to farming. If weeds invade fertile land and compete with the crops for nutrients in the soil and growing space, they will keep farms from being productive. Weeds can spread in many ways. They can be spread by human activity, birds, animals, wind, and water.

Early European settlers in North America unwittingly brought a lot of weed seeds with them. The seeds could have been hidden in the hay they brought over for their animals, in the dirt they used as ballast for their ships, in the fleece and hair of livestock, in their clothes and bedding, or accidentally mixed in with part of the seeds brought over to plant.

Some human activities, such as clearing the land to build on or farm, created open places for weeds to grow. Settlers also purposely brought plants from their countries of origin to reseed areas in their new land, make dye for clothing, or use as ornamental plants (as decorations). Some of these introduced plants may have become weeds.

When plants are introduced to a new environment, they may not have any natural enemies to keep them under control. Because of that, they are not destroyed by disease, insects, or other predators. Without any natural enemies—some of these plants become invasive (grow where they are not wanted) and lower the diversity and quantity of native plants.

Weeds are spreading rapidly in the United States. According to the Bureau of Land Management, in the western United States, weeds are

Facts About Weeds

Purple Loosestrife

- Each flowering stalk can produce 100,000 to 300,000 seeds each year.
- A small cluster can spread and cover a marsh in one growing season.
- Birds and mammals do not eat it, so if it takes over an area, the wildlife habitat is lost.

Knapweed

- One plant produces about 1,000 seeds that can remain fertile for 8 to 20 years.
- The seeds are contained in a fire-resistant stem.
- Some people are allergic to it, and it can irritate their skin.

Leafy Spurge

- Seeds can germinate from 6 inches (15 centimeters) below the surface of the ground.
- Roots can be found 15 feet (4.5 meters) in the ground.
- The milky juice in the leaves and stems is poisonous to most livestock.
- The seed capsules explode when they are dry and can shoot the seeds as far as 15 feet (4.5 meters).
- The seeds can still grow after sitting for 8 years or more.

Gorse

- It grows rapidly and lives for more than 15 years.
- The branches have a high oil content, which causes a serious fire hazard.
- It produces about 8,000 hard-coated seeds each year, which are ejected by bursting pods and can lay dormant (not active) in the soil for 40 years or more.
- Burning and cutting gorse does not get rid of it but rather encourages it to grow more.
- It forces the native vegetation out and is very difficult to control once it takes over an area.

Source: British Columbia Forest Service

spreading roughly 4,000 acres (more than 6 square miles or 15.5 square kilometers) each day on public lands. They are also spreading on private lands, including agricultural farming areas. Although some weeds have beautiful flowers, they can cause serious ecological damage. Weeds take over important habitat areas for wildlife, destroying shelter and nutrients and reducing the number and type of native plants that can grow in the area.

When weeds do not hold or protect the soil the way native plants do, erosion increases, causing sediments to build up in streams. This in turn can hurt fish populations and water quality.

Some weeds, called noxious weeds, are a health hazard for humans or animals because they are poisonous. For example, leafy spurge can cause blindness, skin irritation, and blisters. Hemlock is poisonous and can cause death. Other weeds are hallucinogenic and can cause death, and many cause allergic reactions in people. Weeds also pose a problem in controlling wildfires. Generally, they are less resistant to wildfire than native plants. Weeds also reduce the value of the land. They have a huge impact on ranching and agricultural activities because they can reduce the production of crops. Weeds are a problem all across the country, and controlling them can be very difficult. Once farmers, ranchers, and others realize there is a weed **infestation**, it is usually big enough that it is hard and expensive to eradicate. Biological control (using organisms such as introduced insects or diseases to reduce populations) is effective in slowing the spread of weeds, but it usually cannot get rid of all the weeds. Farmers and ranchers can pull the weeds by hand or use machines to dig them up, but this is usually only done with small infestations. When farmers pull weeds, they must be careful that they do not accidentally spread any new seeds. Herbicides are also good for controlling weeds and stopping their spread when they are found early. Most land managers use an integrated approach, using a combination of these methods.

It is important in agriculture, ranching, and other activities to learn about weeds and get rid of them. A natural functioning ecosystem can easily be thrown out of balance by an invading species. Controlling weeds usually involves the help of several people. It involves awareness, detection, prevention, planning, treatment, coordination, and monitoring to solve the problem.

Examples of invasive weeds include purple loosestrife (in the eastern and western United States); spotted knapweed (in the eastern and western

Weed Multiplication

In order to understand the severity of the invasive weed problem and the rapid expansion of weed communities, we will look at the rate of reproduction of one knapweed during the course of 10 years. We will assume that 100 knapweed seeds are dropped in an area at one time. A knapweed plant produces 1,000 seeds per plant. Of the knapweed seeds, 4% will germinate (sprout) each year, leaving 96% for the following year's seed bank. Of this, 25% of the seedlings that sprout will survive to become mature plants. The knapweed seeds remain viable (able to germinate) for 8 years. It takes 1 year for knapweed to germinate and produce seed. Knapweed plants live for 5 years. The following table shows how many plants and seeds will be produced over the area in the next 10 years:

Year	Plants	Seeds
0	0	100
1	1	1,096
2	12	13,052
3	143	155,530
4	1,698	1,847,309
5	20,071	21,944,417
6	239,614	260,680,640
7	2,846,408	3,096,661,414
8	33,812,879	36,785,673,858
9	401.667,920	436,982,165,807
10	4,771,469,402	5,190,972,273,123

More than 5 billion seeds in 10 years—that means a lot of weeds!

Data supplied courtesy of the U.S. Bureau of Land Management

United States), which can produce 1,000 seeds per plant and whose seeds can lay dormant for eight years; leafy spurge (in the northern United States), which has a powerful root system that can penetrate 25 feet (7.6 meters) deep; yellow starthistle (mainly in the western United States); dalmatian toadflax; garlic mustard, which threatens native spring wildflowers; Oriental bittersweet (in the eastern United States), which is a twining vine that can smother trees and saplings; water hyacinth, which clogs aquatic ecosystems; and melaleuca, a tree that has invaded the Florida Everglades.

The diversity of our native plant communities is decreasing as ecosystems are being damaged by weeds. As native vegetation is reduced, so is the amount of **forage** available for wildlife and livestock.

LAND STEWARDSHIP—MAINTAINING THE HEALTH OF PRIVATELY OWNED LAND

Land stewardship is the concept that people must take care of the land now as well as in the future. Being a steward of the land means taking responsibility for the land and managing it for its long-term welfare. This is no small task. Sometimes it is hard enough to make decisions about issues affecting the present. It is even harder to plan for 5, 10, 15, or 20 years into the future and to take action for the land's welfare now.

Just as a student who looks toward his or her future and wants to end up with a good career takes preparatory steps to achieve that goal, so too must stewards of the land plan ahead. A student prepares for his or her future career by taking classes in middle school and high school that build a foundation and then continuing on to college and refining the training. By the time all the classes have been completed and it is time to graduate, the student is finally ready for the career whose plans began to take shape years before. Similarly, land stewardship involves planning ahead and taking care of the land's natural resources so that they will be available for future generations to use and enjoy. For example, if humans do not take care of the quality of our water today, then 10 years from now it might be too polluted to use. If farmers overfarm the land and make the soil worthless, future generations will not be able to farm it.

Farmers today must meet the needs of the present without compromising the ability of future generations to meet their own needs. Stewardship of the land and its natural resources involves managing it so that the same resources are there for the long term. Leaving the condition of the resources in even better shape than when we got them is the ultimate goal.

Like anything, this involves a plan. People must be educated and records must be kept on management techniques so that future generations can use—or improve on—those techniques. With effective stewardship of the land, humans get many benefits: fertile soils, an abundance of crops, safe drinking water, clear streams, lakes full of fish, skies full of birds, and beautiful landscapes.

Land stewardship began in the United States in 1935, after the devastation of the **Dust Bowl**. The nation made a historic commitment to the stewardship of private land by passing the Soil Conservation Act. Generations today are benefiting from the positive steps of land stewardship started 70 years ago. Just as in the Dust Bowl days, everyone is in this together, and each of us must take part in land stewardship if it is to succeed. The ultimate goal is, through our personal actions, to leave the land in better condition than we found it.

THE HISTORY OF AMERICAN FARMING

A merican farmers today are **conservationists**. They need to be, because the land is their livelihood. It did not always used to be that way, however. Many mistakes and learning experiences over the past 200 years helped to shape current farming into what it has become. Farmers are still learning—still working at having the best relationship they can with the land. This chapter takes a look at the history of American farming and the tragic events that occurred before the concept of land stewardship came into being.

THE DEVELOPMENT AND EVOLUTION OF FARMING IN AMERICA

Farmers made up about 90% of the American workforce in the late eighteenth and early nineteenth centuries. A lot of early American farming techniques came from practices used at that time in England (because many new immigrants to the United States came from England).

Workers pick string beans in a field in Muskogee, Oklahoma, in June 1939. *(Courtesy of the U.S. Department of Agriculture; photo by Russell Lee)*

The **farmer's year** begins in the spring as soon as the ground can be plowed—usually around March. Fields are plowed, seeds are planted, and crops are cultivated and tended until they are ready to be harvested. Depending on the crop, harvests usually happen in late summer or early fall. Some crops, like alfalfa and hay, are able to be harvested earlier—sometimes early enough so that another crop can be planted and harvested in the same growing season.

Manual farming required a lot of people to plow, plant, and harvest the crops. The farm's prosperity depended greatly on the skill of the plowing. Plowing is very hard work, and no other farm activity required so much experience and judgment. The farmers had to know when to plow, how deep to plow, and where to set the first furrow (plowed row). The farmer gained this knowledge by understanding the soil, the terrain, and the characteristics of the future crop.

Physically, plowing was a tremendous challenge. The farmer had to keep 400 pounds (181 kilograms) of wood and steel steady at a consistent depth while walking in uneven, soft soil. It was often a balancing act to keep the plow level and the horses that pulled it in a straight line.

Once a field was plowed, it needed to be planted. The early farmer sowed (planted) seeds by hand as he walked along the length of the furrows, keeping his pace steady and trying to scatter the same amount of seed everywhere. Oftentimes, the seeds were measured into sacks and set at the ends of the furrows so the person sowing knew how many seeds to plant along a given row. The farmer would count his steps and estimate how much seed needed to be scattered with each step.

By 1850, the population of the United States had grown significantly, yet only 64% of the workforce was employed in agriculture. The farmers in the original 13 colonies began to push their way westward to the Great Plains, looking for more land to farm.

The American West provided large areas of land for raising crops and livestock, so the expansion westward rapidly continued. Once farmers began to farm the West, they realized that the arid climate (hot and dry) made the use of new, large-scale farming methods necessary. Farmers in the West were able to grow fruit, vegetables, and wheat as well as raise cattle.

By 1870, the demands of western farming triggered the fast growth of the farm equipment industry. Farms were getting too big to be able to perform all the labor manually. Once farmers had this equipment, they began farming even bigger pieces of land. Between 1870 and 1900, more land was turned into farms than in the 250 years before that. During the late 1800s, there was also a large increase in ranching and the cattle industry. Ranchers grazed their cattle on western prairies and hired cowboys to help manage and drive their herds.

In the early 1900s, because of the dry climate, western farmers had to work a lot of land in order to make any money. In 1909, the U.S. Congress passed the Enlarged Homestead Act, which allowed settlers in the arid western states to own larger pieces of land. That time until the 1920s became known as the Golden Age in agriculture; according to the U.S. Library of Congress, farmers made twice as much money, and the value of their farms increased by 300%.

Machines that could automatically plant seeds (called seed drills) were developed, making life a little easier for farmers. Later, even more sophisticated planting machines appeared. These machines served as mowers, reapers, harvesters, and thrashers. In 1912, the auto plow was invented. It was a tractor with the plow blades already mounted to the bottom of the tractor. The first tractors with enclosed cabs appeared in the late 1930s, further modernizing farming. Today, plows are pulled by large tractors and can cover large tracts of land in a single day.

Today, most aspects of farming are mechanized, but there are still farmers in America who maintain the traditional farm practices from centuries ago. These are the Mennonite farmers of Indiana, Illinois, Ohio, and Pennsylvania. They have preserved the American farming tradition, and through hard work and dedication, they work with the land for its bounty.

THE U.S. DEPARTMENT OF AGRICULTURE

In 1791, President George Washington received a letter from an Englishman named Arthur Young. Mr. Young was looking for information on land values, crops, yields, livestock prices, and taxes. George Washington did not have the answers, so he decided to conduct a mail survey to ask farmers for the information and then compile a report on the results.

After waiting for several months to get the farmers' responses back in the mail, Washington was able to get enough information together to reply to Arthur Young and answer his questions. This report, prepared by George Washington, became the United States' first agricultural survey. It detailed agricultural information for an area 250 miles (402 kilometers) from north to south and 100 miles (161 kilometers) from east to west—an area that lies in Pennsylvania, West Virginia, Virginia, Maryland, and Washington, D.C.

George Washington was very concerned about conservation of farmland. He stressed that farmers should continue to improve their land instead of exhausting (overusing) it. His concerns were very similar to the concerns farmers have today. He worried that prices were not keeping up with what it was costing to grow the crops, and farmers were losing money. He worried that some farmers were not taking care of their land. He also worried about the cost of transporting agricultural goods to markets and improving transportation routes so that farmers did not lose their profits.

George Washington also criticized many farmers for taking the abundance of land they had to work with for granted and not caring for it properly. Unfortunately, American farmers had to learn the hard way that this resource was not limitless, although back then it probably seemed to be.

In 1796, George Washington suggested that a National Board of Agriculture be formed in order to serve farmers better, but Congress rejected the idea. The next major step in American agriculture did not happen until 1839. Commissioner of Patents Henry Ellsworth, convinced Congress to designate $1,000 from the Patent Office Fund for collecting and distributing seeds and collecting data about the country's farms.

A year later, in 1840, a great deal of agricultural information was collected through the first official Census of Agriculture, which provided agricultural information about the entire country. When Ellsworth received the **census** information, he combined it with other information he had collected and was able to estimate the agricultural production of each state and territory. His estimates began the pattern that the government still follows today for annual agricultural reports.

Abraham Lincoln established the U.S. Department of Agriculture (USDA) in 1862. He called it the People's Department. The USDA's first official crop report was published in 1863. At that time, the USDA created a Division of Statistics. During the Civil War, the USDA collected and published crop and livestock statistics to help farmers determine what their goods were worth. Back then, the merchants who bought the products from farmers knew more about critical market information than the farmers themselves. Because of that, farmers were taken advantage of and did not make as much money as they needed to. Statistics still keep farmers from being cheated today.

The USDA's Crop Reporting Board was a very important development. It established a nationwide statistics service for agriculture, which is now called the National Agricultural Statistics Service (NASS).

Today, American agriculture is always being counted and measured, and prices are analyzed and reported so that people have meaningful information. NASS conducts weekly, monthly, quarterly (every three months), and annual (yearly) surveys. It also conducts a five-year census of agriculture (from 1840 to 1920, it was only taken every 10 years). The surveys collect information about all kinds of subjects, such as production and current supplies of food and livestock as well as farmers' incomes. Land use and ownership, the amount of irrigated land, fertilizers and chemicals used, and types of machinery and equipment used are also determined from the surveys. The surveys provide current information about production, economics, and environmental topics. The five-year census of agriculture is the most comprehensive, detailed information-gathering program for agriculture anywhere. NASS is often referred to as the Fact Finders of Agriculture. Besides helping the farmer get a fair price for products he or she produces, the Census of Agriculture data helps the United States plan for the future by having a safe and secure food supply.

THE REALITY OF OVERUSE AND EROSION

Erosion is the process of wearing away the surface of the land. It has always taken place, and always will, because it is a natural process. The surface of the Earth is constantly changing; mountains are lifted up, and streams begin to erode them away; valleys are cut deeper by rivers, and coastlines change with the action of the oceans.

While certain aspects of erosion are actually helpful—it is through erosion processes that soils are formed—some types of erosion can be very damaging to the land. Soil erosion caused by human activity is one of the most destructive erosional forces. Because artificially created erosion can happen much more quickly than natural geologic erosion, it is sometimes referred to as *accelerated erosion.*

Human activity on the landscape can significantly contribute to soil erosion. In a natural state, vegetation serves as natural protection against erosion because the network of roots helps hold the soil in place against various erosive forces, such as wind and water. Scientists estimate that, in the United States, 30% of erosion is due to natural forces and 70% is due to human impact. Oftentimes, when people use the land for farming and **overgrazing**, the protective covering of natural vegetation is destroyed, and the erosion process speeds up. In fact, studies have shown that artificially created erosion played a big part in the downfall of many early civilizations. Poor land management practices degraded the soil until it was no longer productive enough to support the population living in the area. Early civilizations that recognized the disastrous effects of erosion used devices such as **terracing** the land to keep from plowing, planting, and irrigating on hillside slopes where water could wash the fertile soil away.

There are many causes of erosion. It can occur by wind, water, drought, overfarming, lack of **ground cover**, and overgrazing. Erosion by wind is worse in arid and semiarid areas. It removes soil and natural vegetation and causes dryness and deterioration of the soil structure.

Water erosion is greatest when heavy rainstorms fall on land that is unprotected by vegetation. Some soils are more easily eroded than others. *Rill erosion* occurs when many tiny water channels are formed. *Interrill* erosion happens when a layer of soil is removed. *Gully erosion* happens when thin water columns quickly remove the soil from an area. *Saltation erosion* is the removal of soil and minerals by wind, water, or gravity.

Overuse and erosion of the land can rob the soil of valuable nutrients, making it unproductive. Every year in the United States, thousands of acres of **arable land** are lost. Between 1990 and 2000, the United States lost almost 44 million acres of arable land. Some of this land was lost because homes, parking lots, and other structures were

Unchecked water erosion in a field. *(Courtesy of the U.S. Department of Agriculture; photo by Ron Nichols)*

built on it; some of the land was polluted by industrial water and other pollutants; some of the land blew away or washed away; and some of the land was lost because it had been used to produce food year after year for too many years. Once the land has been overused or eroded, it is often nonrenewable because soil takes too long to re-form. This is one of the most important issues in land stewardship.

THE DUST BOWL OF THE 1930S

It took many years and the extensive erosion and loss of valuable agricultural soil before American farmers learned the lesson that George Washington was trying to teach back in 1788. The worst loss of agricultural soil in American history occurred during the early 1900s.

During World War I (1914-1918), there were significant wheat shortages, which caused the price of wheat to rise dramatically. At that time, wheat was very profitable—farmers could make a lot of money selling it. The U.S. government encouraged farmers to produce more wheat, so farmers on the fragile southern Great Plains plowed up the natural grass cover, which had protected the soil for centuries, to plant winter wheat. The Great Plains extend eastward from the Rocky Mountains across the western parts of North Dakota, South Dakota, Nebraska, Kansas, Oklahoma, and Texas.

Soon, the wheat crops exhausted the topsoil. In addition, overgrazing by cattle and sheep herds stripped the western plains of their protective grass cover. Then the area was devastated by a severe drought from 1934 to 1937. Because the land had been plowed up, and the delicate, stabilizing root systems formed by the grass removed, the large plowed areas had nothing to keep them anchored in place. A lot of the soil dried out, turned to dust, and blew away. The area was covered with horrible dust storms and sandstorms that buried roads, houses, towns, and fields. Clouds of dust were blown as far away as Chicago, New York, and Washington, D.C. It turned the skies dark. Eventually, the soil blew out over the Atlantic Ocean, where it was lost forever.

This area was called the Dust Bowl. It covered an area 500 miles (805 kilometers) by 300 miles (483 kilometers) in size—almost 100 million

The Dust Bowl of the 1930s. A dust storm approaches Stratford, Texas, in April 1935. *(Courtesy of the USDA Wind Erosion Research Unit; photo by George E. Marsh)*

acres of land. The drought and topsoil loss lasted until 1938. Many people who lived in the Dust Bowl states abandoned their farms and moved away. The Dust Bowl exodus was the largest migration in American history. By 1940, 2.5 million people had moved out of the Great Plains.

In response to this disaster, the federal government created the Soil Erosion Service (SES) and the Civilian Conservation Corps (CCC) to recover the land. Many conservation practices were begun, such as replanting the grass, planting tree windbreaks (called **shelter belts**), crop rotation, **contour plowing**, and **strip plowing**. The SES and CCC also showed farmers new scientific agricultural methods to help them protect the fragile ecosystem of the Southern Plains. The historian Robert Worster wrote the following about this period:

The ultimate meaning of the dust storms of the 1930s was that America as a whole, not just the Plains, was badly out of balance with its natural environment. Unbounded optimism about the future, careless disregard of nature's limits and uncertainties, uncritical faith in Providence, devotion to self-aggrandizement—all these were national as well as regional characteristics.

Today, decades of conservation methods have begun to pay off. The erosion rate by water has decreased, farmers are consistently using conservation practices, and more farmland is being enrolled in the **Conservation Reserve Program** every year. This program, run by the U.S. Department of Agriculture, provides technical and financial assistance to farmers and ranchers to help them manage their lands in an environmentally friendly and cost-effective manner. It helps farmers and ranchers reduce soil erosion, provide for the nation's food sources, and help improve water quality.

Case Study: Conservation In Action

People involved in agriculture throughout the country are always looking for new and innovative ways to conserve natural resources and improve farming techniques. For example, farmers in the northeastern United States began looking for a way to extend the growing season so they could produce food longer. Some are now using high tunnels. These are simple plastic-covered structures that keep crops warm and sheltered. High tunnels resemble greenhouses, but they cost must less to build and operate. To make a high tunnel, a farmer stretches a layer of clear plastic sheeting over a metal pipe frame about 20 by 100 feet (6 by 30 meters) in size. The structures are easy to use, and the plastic sides can even be rolled up to allow fresh air to circulate around the crops. Farmers have been able to add weeks—sometimes months—to their growing season to produce more food. Fruits, vegetables, and flowers can be grown in high tunnels. Some farmers grow their produce organically, without any agrochemicals.

THE SOIL CONSERVATION ACT

Hugh Hammond Bennett, a soil scientist and member of President Franklin D. Roosevelt's administration, realized that every American's future was tied to the plight of the Dust Bowl farmers. It affected the entire country, not just the Great Plains. He wanted to preserve the soil by reforming farming practices. He became known as the Father of Soil Conservation.

In 1933, Bennett became the first director of the newly formed Soil Erosion Service, whose job it was to fight against erosion and improve farming methods. Through his work and efforts, the Soil Conservation Act of 1935 was passed. Its focus was on improving farming techniques.

The Soil Conservation Act established the **Soil Conservation Service (SCS)**. The chief purpose of this agency was to deal with issues of soil erosion. Bennett was largely responsible for the acceptance of workable soil conservation methods. He played a major role in converting a large part of the Great Plains back to grasslands. In 1943, he wrote in the *Annals of the Association of American Geographers*: "If we are bold in our thinking, courageous in accepting new ideas, and willing to work with, instead of against, our land, we shall find in conservation farming an avenue to the greatest food production the world has ever known—not only for the war, but for the peace that is to follow." In its early years, the SCS conducted soil surveys of land around the United States. It also looked at other conservation problems, such as **soil salinity control**. The SCS currently publishes maps showing areas of soil erosion and is also involved in the scientific research of pesticides. Without the help of the SCS, Americans probably would not have come as far as they have today in rehabilitating and taking care of the land.

RENEWABLE AND NONRENEWABLE RESOURCES

There are two general classes of resources: renewable and nonrenewable. This chapter focuses on the various agricultural resources and the important cycles that affect them. The relationship of these resources within the food chain is also explored. Agricultural resources including soil, crops, livestock, and aquatic resources are also addressed.

WHY SOME AGRICULTURAL RESOURCES ARE RENEWABLE AND SOME ARE NOT

A **renewable resource** is a resource that can be replenished. It is a resource that can be replaced through natural ecological cycles or good management practices. The opposite of this is a nonrenewable resource—a resource that cannot be replenished (once it is gone, it is gone for good). For practical applications, some scientists consider a renewable resource one that can be replenished within one generation (approximately 20 to 30 years) and a nonrenewable resource one that cannot be replenished in one generation.

For many classes of resources, it is easy to determine which resources are renewable and which are not. For example, with energy resources, fossil fuels (oil, petroleum) and coal are not renewable because they took millions of years to form. Even though the same geological processes are still happening today, these resources will not be replaced within our lifetime, so they are considered nonrenewable. Energy resources, such as wind power and water power, are considered renewable because they are readily abundant and can be generated on a nearly continual basis. When looking at agricultural resources, soil might be considered a nonrenewable resource (as discussed in Chapter 1) because it takes hundreds of years to form. Determining whether agricultural resources are renewable or nonrenewable is not as clear-cut as for other types of resources, like energy.

Agricultural resources involve ecosystems, which are fragile and complex. All elements of living systems are interwoven; if one element is affected, the entire system is affected. Compare these interactions to a car: A car will work well as long as all the individual components are being taken care of and functioning right; but, if suddenly, one of the parts is neglected and stops working properly— for example, if the car runs out of gas—it impacts the entire system. If one component stops working the way it should, the entire system is jeopardized, and until that one component is managed correctly, the system fails or is unproductive.

America saw this happen with the Dust Bowl—the soil system was damaged, which triggered a chain reaction, making the land unfarmable. Using soil too much over a long period of time for a single crop can rob it of the specific nutrients needed by that crop. If the nutrients in the soil are used up, then any crop requiring those nutrients will be unable to grow. If the delicate balance is affected, that crop can become nonrenewable.

Another form of nonrenewability concerns invasive plants and noxious weeds. If an aggressive plant or weed infests an area, it can crowd out native plants by using vital nutrients in the soil so that the native plants cannot survive. If the invasive plant takes over, the native plant becomes nonrenewable in that area as long as those conditions exist.

Concerning animals, if the land cannot support an animal population, then the animal resource is no longer available in that area. For example, if ranchers permit cattle to overgraze, that destroys the soil and grass systems and prevents further grazing. The balance can be so upset, in fact, that a process called **desertification** can take place, making the area uninhabitable for plants, animals, and even people.

So, while many people may think that fruits, vegetables, grains, flowers, trees, and animals are automatically renewable—that is not necessarily so. Their availability is part of a complex system that must be delicately balanced. The key to understanding this system is to understand six important natural cycles that exist on Earth.

THE SIX CRITICAL RESOURCE CYCLES: MAINTAINING A DELICATE BALANCE

The six cycles that work together are the water, nitrogen, carbon, phosphorus, oxygen, and energy cycles.

The Water Cycle

Water is necessary for plant growth, for dissolving and transporting plant nutrients, and for the survival of soil organisms. The water cycle is fundamental to all life on Earth.

From a fast-moving stream, to a rainfall, to movement of water through the ground, water is always in motion. The endless movement and recycling of water between the atmosphere, the land's surface, and underground is called the water cycle, or the hydrologic cycle.

Two separate forces make the water cycle work. The energy of the sun and the force of the Earth's gravity drive it. Water vapor is carried through the atmosphere by air currents. When the air cools, it condenses, forming clouds. Some of the moisture falls back to Earth as rain, snow, hail, or sleet.

Once the water reaches the ground, it can go in several directions before it returns again to the atmosphere. Plants can use the water, it can be stored in lakes, or it can seep into the soil. The sun's energy can then make the water evaporate back into the atmosphere, or the Earth's gravity can pull the water that has entered the ground down through the soil to be stored for years as slowly moving groundwater.

Groundwater can be stored in aquifers (natural underground reservoirs) or it can eventually seep into springs and resurface. Water on the surface is returned to the atmosphere through the process of **evaporation**. Water that has been used by plants is returned to the atmosphere as vapor through **transpiration**, which happens when water passes through the leaves of plants. These two concepts together are called **evapotranspiration**. Evapotranspiration is greatest in areas that are hot, dry, sunny, or windy.

The presence of water in agriculture and grazing must be well managed. Although water is critical for plant growth and transporting nutrients, it can also be a destructive force if not managed properly. It can cause soil compaction, which clumps the particles of soil close together and removes the important air space needed for nutrients to move through the soil; it can leach (remove) nutrients from the soil; and too much water can cause excess runoff and erosion.

The Nitrogen Cycle

The nitrogen cycle is the process by which nitrogen in the atmosphere enters the soil and becomes part of living organisms, before returning to the atmosphere. Nitrogen makes up 78% of the Earth's atmosphere. This nitrogen must, however, be converted from a gas into a chemically usable form before living organisms can use it. This transformation takes place through the nitrogen cycle, which transforms the nitrogen gas into ammonia or nitrates.

Most of the nitrogen conversion process occurs biologically. This is done by free-living, nitrogen-fixing bacteria; bacteria living on the roots of plants; and through certain algae and lichens.

Nitrogen that has been converted to ammonia and nitrates is used directly by plants and is absorbed in their tissues as plant proteins. The nitrogen then passes from plants to herbivores (plant-eating animals) and then to carnivores (meat-eating animals).

When plants and animals die, the nitrogen compounds are broken down by decomposing into ammonia. Some of this ammonia is then used by plants, and the rest is either dissolved or held in the soil. If it is dissolved or held in the soil, microorganisms then go to work on it in a process called *nitrification*. Nitrates can be stored in humus or washed from the soil and carried away to streams and lakes. Nitrates may also be converted and returned to the atmosphere by a process called *denitrification*.

The nitrogen cycle is important because plants need nitrogen to grow, develop, and produce seeds. The main source of nitrogen in soils is from organic matter (humus). Bacteria living in the soil convert organic forms of nitrogen to inorganic forms that plants can use. Nitrogen is then taken up by plant roots. When the plant dies, it decays and becomes part of the organic matter in the soil. The land must be well managed or nitrogen can be washed out of the soil, which then impacts the growth of crops.

The Carbon Cycle

The carbon cycle is important because carbon is the basic structural material for all cell life. Carbon makes the soil productive, and plants healthy. The carbon cycle is the movement of carbon between the atmosphere, the oceans, the land, and living organisms.

The atmosphere and plants exchange carbon. Plants absorb carbon dioxide from the atmosphere during **photosynthesis** and then release carbon dioxide back into the atmosphere during respiration. Another major exchange of carbon dioxide happens between the oceans and the atmosphere. The dissolved carbon dioxide in the oceans is used by ocean plants in photosynthesis.

Carbon is also exchanged through the soil. Crop and animal residues decompose and form organic matter, which contains carbon.

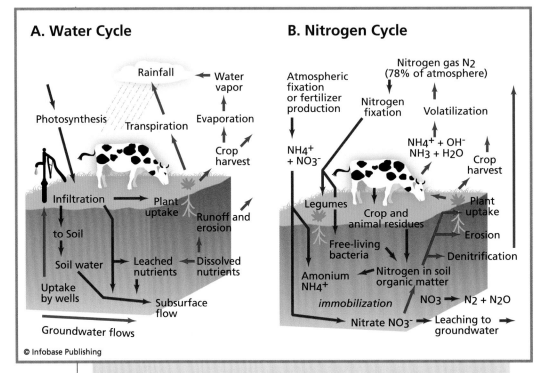

A. Water Cycle

Rainfall — Water vapor
Photosynthesis
Transpiration   Evaporation
Crop harvest
Infiltration   Plant uptake   Runoff and erosion
to Soil
Soil water   Leached nutrients ← Dissolved nutrients
Uptake by wells
Subsurface flow
Groundwater flows

© Infobase Publishing

B. Nitrogen Cycle

Nitrogen gas N2 (78% of atmosphere)
Atmospheric fixation or fertilizer production   Nitrogen fixation   Volatilization
NH4+ + OH-
NH3 + H2O
NH4+ + NO3-   Crop harvest
Legumes   Crop and animal residues   Plant uptake
Free-living bacteria   Erosion
Amonium NH4+   Nitrogen in soil organic matter   Denitrification
immobilization   NO3 → N2 + N2O
Nitrate NO3- → Leaching to groundwater

(A) The Water Cycle: Water repeatedly moves through the atmosphere, ground surface, and ground subsurface to support life systems on Earth.
(B) The Nitrogen Cycle: Plant and animal wastes decompose and add nitrogen to the soil. The bacteria in the soil converts the nitrogen into forms that plants can use; plants use the nitrogen in the soil to grow; people and animals eat the plants; then animal and plant residues return nitrogen to the soil again, completing the cycle.

For plants to be able to use these nutrients, soil organisms break them down in a process called *mineralization.*

Animals also give off carbon dioxide when they breathe. Some plants are eaten by grazing animals, which then return organic carbon to the soil as manure. Easily broken-down forms of carbon in manure and plant cells are released as carbon dioxide. Forms of carbon that are difficult to break down become stabilized in the soil as humus.

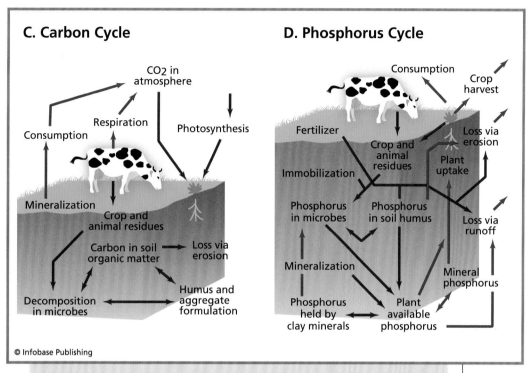

C. Carbon Cycle

D. Phosphorus Cycle

© Infobase Publishing

(C) The Carbon Cycle: Plants take up carbon dioxide through photosynthesis. Animals eat the plants. They then give off carbon dioxide to the atmosphere as well as organic carbon to the soil in manure. Carbon is used by plants from the soil through mineralization. Other carbon remains in the soil as humus.

(D) The Phosphorus Cycle: Soil organisms mineralize (release) phosphorus from organic matter. Plants use the phosphorus. Animals eat the plants. Animals either use the phosphorus or return it to the soil.

The Phosphorus Cycle

Like nitrogen, phosphorus is a primary plant nutrient. Phosphorus is not part of the atmosphere, however. It is found in rocks, minerals, and organic matter in the soil. Chemical reactions and activity by microbes (microorganisms) in the soil affect the availability of phosphorus for plants to use.

Plants use phosphorus for energy and reproduction. Animals consume phosphorus when they eat plants. The phosphorus that is not used to help the animal grow is returned to the soil in the animal's manure. Once the phosphorus is in the soil again, it is decomposed by soil organisms so that it can be used by plants again, and the cycle repeats itself.

The Oxygen Cycle

The oxygen cycle follows the same paths as the carbon cycle because oxygen is part of carbon dioxide. Oxygen is also present in water. Oxygen is released to the atmosphere during plant photosynthesis.

The Energy Cycle

The energy cycle is powered by sunlight, which plants convert into carbohydrates. In order to capture as much solar energy as possible, plants need to be very dense (growing close together). The angle of leaves also has an effect on the energy they can absorb. Taller plants are able to capture more sunlight. Plants with horizontal leaves capture more sunlight than grasses with vertical (upright) leaves.

Energy from plants is transferred into the soil by the death and decay of plant roots and matter, which eventually decompose enough to become humus. During these steps, energy is being used in the decomposition or is lost as heat.

Thick, green plants create a high-energy flow. When livestock animals eat the plants, they become the next link in the energy cycle. Livestock convert the plant material into meat, milk, and fiber. Animal manure gets recycled through decomposition in the ground. The energy cycle is necessary to have the highest efficiency of fertile rangelands.

All of these cycles are important to the success of agriculture. If any of them are interrupted or damaged, the others are impacted as well, because the different cycles share common components, such as soil, plants, or animals.

If these cycles get interrupted or destroyed, it can become impossible to grow certain crops or raise certain animals. This, in turn, relates back to the renewability and nonrenewability of resources and the delicate balance that must be maintained for a healthy ecosystem.

FOOD WEBS

Maintaining a healthy balance has a direct impact on food chains and food webs. A food chain is the path of food energy from the producer (plant source) through the hierarchy of consumers (animals). For example, if grass is at the beginning of the chain, it may then be eaten by a grasshopper. The chain continues as a mouse eats the grasshopper, a snake eats the mouse, and finally, an eagle eats the snake. In this example, grass is at the bottom of the food chain, and the eagle is at the top (assuming nothing eats the eagle).

The real world is much more complex than a simple food chain, however. There might be a few organisms whose diet includes only one item, but that is not usually the case. For example, the eagle eats snakes, but it also eats many other things (squirrels, rodents, and rabbits), and those other things are part of food chains as well. A more complex and realistic way of looking at these processes is through a food web. A food web consists of many interconnected food chains. The only way to untangle the chain is to trace a specific food chain back to its source.

Food webs are critical in agriculture, both in cultivating crops in fields, and in grazing animals on rangelands. They are also very complex, and like most complex, interconnected systems, the whole is greater than the sum of its parts—if the parts are removed, the system disintegrates. In the food web, if key organisms or multiple groups disappear, the web may collapse.

As food chains move from soils, to plants, to animals, to humans, it is not hard to see why maintaining a working system is important. If any part of these systems fails, then everything up the food web from that point is negatively impacted. Again, this relates back to the renewability and nonrenewability of agricultural resources. If a system or multiple systems are completely destroyed, resources can become nonrenewable.

SOIL RESOURCES

The health of soil resources is related to factors such as fertility, fragility, and erosion. Land use and land management have a tremendous impact on the health of the soil.

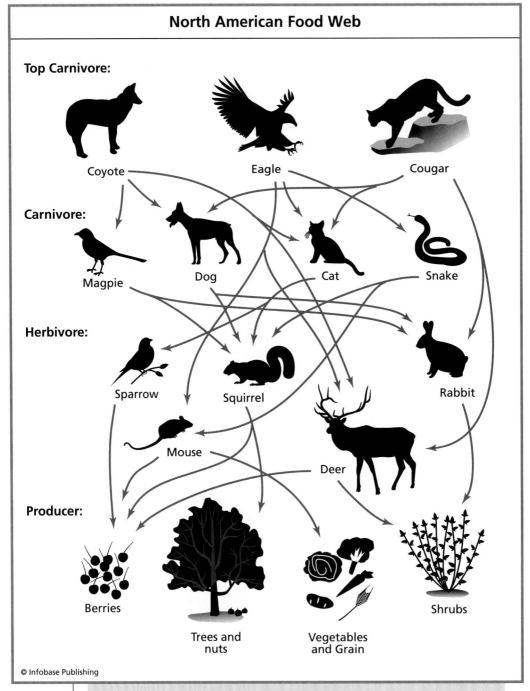

North American Food Web

Top Carnivore:

Coyote   Eagle   Cougar

Carnivore:

Magpie   Dog   Cat   Snake

Herbivore:

Sparrow   Squirrel   Rabbit

Mouse   Deer

Producer:

Berries   Trees and nuts   Vegetables and Grain   Shrubs

An example of a North American food web.

Because soil is a nonrenewable resource (it takes longer than a generation to form), protecting soil quality is very important. Soil is important in many ways: It provides a home to organisms, it decomposes wastes, it filters contaminants from water, it is used to grow crops in, and it plays a role in gas exchange (which keeps the resource cycles going). Because there is a limited amount of soil, it must be properly cared for.

There are several ways that farmers and ranchers take care of this valuable resource—many of which were learned after the Dust Bowl experience. Farmers can reduce the amount of tilling (disturbing and overturning the soil by plowing) that they do on the land. They can practice farming conservation by rotating crops, using buffer strips, keeping fields **fallow**, using compost in the soil, terracing steep land, strip cropping, contour farming, and not overgrazing livestock.

In crop rotation, the farmer grows a series of different crops, one after the other, in the same field. This reduces the threat from pests and disease associated with a particular crop and helps the soil stay fertile and healthy. Leaving land fallow is also helpful. Fallow land is land that is left unplanted so it can recover nutrients that may have been lost from a previous crop. It gives the soil time to rest. Buffer strips, contour farming, and terracing are all conservation techniques that the farmer can use. (These will be discussed further in Chapter 8, which deals with conservation.) In addition, composting can be used to add additional nutrients to the soil (called soil augmentation). Compost is a mixture that is made up of decayed organic matter and is used for fertilizing and conditioning the land.

Ranchers can take care not to overgraze their land, which uses up all the nutrients in the soil. Overgrazing also allows too many cattle to trample an area, squeezing the soil particles together so that there is no open air space. This keeps nutrients and water from being able to move around inside the soil to keep it fertile.

Farmers and ranchers must also control rainfall runoff. Runoff water dissolves nutrients and removes them from the pasture as it flows over the soil surface. Soil erosion transports nutrients away.

It can also move contaminants, such as pesticides, that are attached to soil particles and redeposit them in other places, like rivers or lakes.

CROP RESOURCES

There are many agricultural crops produced in the United States, and different commodities (items) are produced in different parts of the country. The United States is fortunate to have a large variety of crops that can be grown, such as fruits, vegetables, grains, hay,

How Well Do You Know Your Favorite Farm Products?

Potatoes

The potato is not a root but a storage area. The roots collect more water and food than the growing plant can use at one time. The plant stores the excess food in oval packages, called tubers. Tubers are the potatoes. They are green originally, and when they turn brown, they are ready to harvest. They produce more pounds of protein per acre than corn, rice, wheat, or oats. Potatoes were first grown by ancient tribes living in the Andes Mountains of South America in A.D. 200, but people in North America did not start eating them until they became popular in Europe.

Most of the world's potatoes are grown in Europe, but potatoes are also grown in all 50 states. Potatoes grow best in cool mountain areas. The United States' biggest potato producer is Idaho; the second biggest is Washington. The average American eats 125 pounds (56.5 kg) of potatoes or potato products (such as potato chips and french fries) each year.

Apples

Apples have been around for 750,000 years, and there are 8,000 varieties of them. The United States' biggest producer of apples is Washington, followed by New York. An apple tree lives an average of 100 years. Growing a single apple takes a full year. Red apples need

cotton, tobacco, sugar, beans, peas, lentils, flowers, and landscaping plants and trees, just to name a few.

One issue that farmers must contend with is pests—such as infestations of insects. Pests are anything that damages or competes with a crop or plant. Weeds are also considered pests.

If insects are not controlled, they can destroy an entire crop. An example of this occurs when crickets inhabit a wheat field and destroy the crop so that there is nothing left for the farmer to harvest. Another example is the grain weevil. It attacks stored grain,

cool nights during harvest to trigger an enzyme that makes them appear redder in color (called blush).

Wheat
Wheat is one of the oldest known foods. There are more than 30,000 varieties of wheat. It can be grown in many different types of climates. Somewhere in the world, wheat is being harvested every month of the year. Kansas is the biggest producer of wheat in the United States, followed by North Dakota. Winter wheat is planted before September and is not harvested until the following May—it lies dormant during the coldest winter months. In addition to being used in food, wheat is also used to make wallpaper glue and other building products.

Corn
Corn is actually a type of grass. The plants can grow to be 7 to 10 feet (2.1 to 3 meters) tall. There are more than 3,500 different uses for corn products, including oil, syrup, starch, and fructose. It can even be used to produce a fuel for cars, trucks, and buses called ethanol. Most of the corn in the United States is eaten by cattle, sheep, hogs, and poultry. Iowa is the nation's top producer of corn, closely followed by Illinois.

Source: U.S. Department of Agriculture

eating some of it and causing the rest to mold so that it is unusable. Flour mites can contaminate stored flour. Potato blight is a form of fungus that attacks potato leaves. It then gets into the soil and infects the potatoes. Fire blight is a disease that kills fruit trees.

Many farmers use pesticides to control pest infestations. (Pesticides are discussed in more detail in Chapter 5.) Farmers use herbicides to control weed infestations in large areas. When they are applied as sprays, they can reach the weeds growing in with the crop. Herbicides can be used in several ways: on the ground before the crop is planted, in order to kill existing weeds; to kill any existing weeds after the seeds have been sown but before the crop germinates; to kill weeds after the crop is already growing; and to keep new weeds from growing later in the harvest cycle.

Different herbicides are used for different types of weeds—some work on the leaves of weeds, while others work on their root systems. Fungicides are also used. Fungus can attack the roots, leaves, or fruit of plants. Another way to fight pests is through biological controls. This includes the use of natural predators to control insect populations. While more environmentally safe, it has not proven to be as effective as chemical pesticides.

Crops evolve over time. Corn and wheat are both examples of crops that have evolved into better varieties. Corn originally had very small cobs. The cobs were covered with a thin husk that opened easily to let the seeds drop to the ground. Humans altered corn by selecting plants with larger cobs. Over time, the cobs evolved to become tightly wrapped in a thick husk, which is firmly attached to the stalk. This corn was easier for people to harvest.

Wheat has also evolved. Wild wheat has an ear that breaks easily so that its seeds can be carried by the wind. Farmers began selecting plants with the biggest, toughest ears because they were easier to pick. Because of the attention to the larger ears, wheat slowly began to change. New forms began to appear with bigger grains. These different generations of wheat eventually developed into the wheat that farmers harvest today.

Today, farmers have learned how crops grow, identified their strengths and weaknesses, and selectively bred certain varieties with others in order to obtain the best produce. Plant breeders also breed plants that are stronger, have better resistance to disease, and have the potential to produce larger crops.

LIVESTOCK RESOURCES

Animal husbandry is the care and breeding of domesticated animals, such as sheep, cattle, goats, hogs, pigs, and horses. The science of animal husbandry is called *animal science.*

The domestication of wild animals was one of the most significant steps of human civilization in order to shift from a hunter-gatherer lifestyle to an agricultural one. Sheep began to be domesticated around 9000 B.C. Scientists also know that selective breeding of livestock in order to improve its quality existed during Roman times. Through the centuries, farmers have herded and cared for animals. In the United States, after westward expansion, cowboys fulfilled the same role.

Modern-day farming and ranching has become very complex and involved. It takes many professionals to run a farm or ranch. For example, there may be breeders, health specialists, milkers, feeders, and others to care for specific animal needs.

Livestock has also been significantly affected by genetic engineering in order to produce better and stronger animals. By using breeding techniques, such as embryo transfer and artificial insemination, scientists have been able to improve the quality of livestock, which in turn produces more meat, fiber, and milk for humans.

Livestock are used for many purposes. For example, many are used as a supply of meat and dairy products (milk, yogurt, cheese, butter, and ice cream). They are also used to obtain materials such as textiles (wool from sheep) and leather. Fertilizer is an important commodity made from the manure of livestock. Animals can also be used to pull plows and work on farms that do not use mechanized (mechanical) farming practices. On rangeland, grazing animals are

(Top) A Navajo sheep herder in New Mexico. *(Courtesy of the U.S. Department of Agriculture; photo by Ken Hammond)*

(Bottom) A beautiful Navajo hand-woven rug is one example of a fiber product from a rangeland animal. Only certain species of sheep are used to produce these rugs. *(Photo by Julie A. Kerr, Nature's Images)*

often used to control weed growth on open lands. Removing the weeds not only helps the condition of the land but also reduces the risk of wildfire by removing weeds that could likely fuel a wildfire.

There is a diverse range of livestock around the world, raised for a variety of purposes. Animals raised as meat sources include cattle, goats, sheep, bison, deer, goats, donkeys, llamas, pigs, rabbits, water buffalo, hogs, and yaks. Animals that are a reliable source of dairy products include cattle, donkeys, goats, bison, camels, sheep, reindeer, water buffalo, and yaks. Leather comes from pigs, cattle, reindeer, and bison. Wool comes from sheep, alpacas, goats, llamas, rabbits, and yaks.

Farm animals can be raised in large or small enclosures, such as cages, pens, sheds, and barns; in fenced pastures; or on large open ranges depending on the size and needs of the animals. Some people have protested the way animals are sometimes cared for, especially animals kept in feedlots where they live in crowded conditions. Many significant steps have been made over the years to provide for the welfare of animals, and the government regulates and closely monitors livestock operations.

Besides the welfare of animals and their comfort, livestock practices are also regulated and monitored because disease can be quickly spread in livestock areas. If livestock becomes infected, the animals may not only die but also infect other livestock. In addition, certain diseases can be passed on to humans. For example, some infectious diseases throughout history have originated from animals. Cattle have been responsible for the spread of smallpox, measles, and tuberculosis. Pigs have been the source of influenza (the flu) and pertussis (whooping cough).

Mad cow disease has been a problem in some areas, such as Britain. It can also be transmitted to humans if they eat the infected cattle, which can then cause a fatal brain disease called Creutzfeldt-Jakob disease. *Escherichia coli*—a food-borne bacterial illness—can be spread to humans, as well. *E. coli* is often linked to eating undercooked, contaminated ground beef.

Cattle graze on an open range in Montana. *(Courtesy of the Agricultural Research Service; photo by Keith Weller)*

Anthrax is another infectious disease, one that can be contracted from cattle, sheep, goats, antelopes, and camels. Infected soil can also be a source of anthrax. West Nile virus is another disease that can infect livestock, such as horses; significant efforts have been made to control it.

Sometimes, antibiotics are given to livestock to prevent diseases, but the use of antibiotics in animals that end up in the human food chain has created a lot of controversy. Because livestock can be affected by many diseases, veterinary certificates are required before animals can be transported, sold, or exhibited in shows. Even show horses must have certificates in order to move them from one state to another.

Amazing Cow Facts

Did you know . . . ?

- At birth, the average calf weighs 75 to 100 pounds (34 to 45 kilograms).
- A dairy cow weights about 1,500 pounds (680 kilograms).
- A cow has 4 separate compartments in its stomach. The average cow spends 6 to 10 hours a day eating and consumes about 90 pounds (40.8 kilograms) of food.
- A dairy cow drinks 25 to 50 gallons (95 to 189 liters) of water each day—almost a bathtub full.
- Dairy cows can produce 50 to 100 glasses of milk each day. They are milked 2 to 3 times each day.
- Meat comes from beef cattle, and milk comes from dairy cattle. Cattle are also a main source of leather.
- Cattle products are ingredients in some surprising things. Chewing gum has an ingredient in it that comes from cows. Makeup, detergent, floor wax, perfume, and crayons are made from the fats and proteins produced by cattle. Cows also provide a substance called glycerin that helps to fight dental plaque. It is used in toothpaste and mouthwash.
- Texas is the biggest cattle-producing state, followed by Kansas and Nebraska.
- The largest milk producer in the United States is California, followed by Wisconsin.

Source: U.S. Department of Agriculture

AQUATIC RESOURCES

Aquatic resources are food resources obtained from the water, including streams, ponds, lakes, and oceans through **aquaculture**. Aquaculture is the cultivation of aquatic organisms, such as fish, shellfish, algae, and other aquatic plants. Examples of aquaculture include raising catfish in freshwater ponds, farming salmon in net

Catfish farming is a form of aquaculture. *(Courtesy of the U.S. Department of Agriculture; photo by Ken Hammond)*

pens set out in a bay, trout farming, and even "growing" cultured pearls from oysters. Tuna farming is important in Australia.

Today, aquaculture is the fastest-growing sector of U.S. agriculture, as well as global food production. Many people see aquaculture as a solution to the problems fishermen have encountered from years of overfishing certain areas of the oceans, which has resulted in declining fish resources.

Fish farming is the main form of aquaculture. This is an operation where fish are raised in tanks or other types of enclosures, such as ponds. The fish are used mainly for food but are also used to "seed" sport-fishing areas (meaning that fish are supplied to lakes and rivers for people to catch).

Some fish are raised in cages in existing water resources, such as streams and lakes. This system has many advantages; many different types of fish can be raised, and it can be done in the same areas where sport fishing occurs. A disadvantage is the risk of unintentional spread of disease or other contaminants to wild fish populations. Fish that are used to stock lakes and rivers, such as trout, are usually raised from eggs to fingerlings (small fish) and then released into lakes and rivers. They are raised in long, shallow concrete tanks fed with fresh stream water.

Fish farming can raise many species, such as salmon, catfish, tilapia, cod, and trout. Aquaculture is being monitored to look for drawbacks or problems. One of the largest problems is that it requires a lot of water—nearly a million gallons of water per acre. Because of this, scientists have developed ways to recycle the water.

Another issue that is being closely monitored is the potential for the spread of invasive species. Similar to invasive weeds, farmed fish species can escape into open water and compete with native species for limited resources. If an invasive species competes with a native species, it can damage the ecosystem of that area. Another issue is the possibility of diseases being spread by farmed fish species. Nevertheless, aquaculture could prove to be a significant resource to support growing populations in the years to come.

4

DEVELOPMENT OF AGRICULTURAL DIVERSITY

This chapter examines the diversity of farming techniques and the most common agricultural methods, as well as the science of biotechnology and how it affects us today and into the future.

TYPES OF FARMS

As farming has developed and advanced over the years, different farming techniques have evolved. Farmers have learned from experiences—like the Dust Bowl in the 1930s—and devised more efficient ways to manage the land. In order to be able to produce a lot of food and keep it as inexpensive as possible for the consumer, developed countries like the United States have had to use pesticides (to kill insects), fertilizers (to make the soil more productive), and mechanized production (machines like combines, balers, and **tillers.**) With the help of these techniques, farmers in America are able to produce enough food for the millions of people who are not farmers.

Farmers have realized for a long time how important it is to protect natural resources, like soil, water, and biological (living) resources. Because of this, most farmers are good stewards of the land. As populations continue to increase, however, more demands are made on the land and on farmers. As resources get overused, the quality of the environment can be negatively impacted, which is why farmers are increasingly turning to concepts like land stewardship in order to protect the land for the future.

Many people recognize that, in order to protect our natural resources, there must be government regulations, incentive programs for those that manage the land, and farming techniques that keep the land healthy. Farmers recognize that farming has specific environmental effects on the land. When land is converted to agricultural use, it loses much of its **biodiversity** (ability to support many different types of living things) and habitats. Erosion can occur when fields are plowed, which causes soil to be damaged and lost. The supply of water can be reduced for other purposes, and water quality can be impacted.

The effects of agriculture also touch areas outside the farm. For example, the water supply over a broad area can be impacted if a great deal of water is needed for irrigation. Existing habitats can be destroyed when land use is changed. Agriculture can also alter chemical cycles and climatic conditions.

Soils are affected by agricultural production. When the natural vegetation is cleared for agriculture, soils can become eroded and soil fertility can be lessened. When the aboveground vegetation cover is removed, the plant roots are also destroyed and can no longer protect and stabilize the soil. Soils that are disturbed by plowing are also more easily eroded by water and wind. There are about 17,000 different soil types recognized worldwide. How easily a particular soil erodes depends on many factors, such as soil type, how steep the land is, the amount of organic matter present in the soil, and how intensive the erosion processes are.

One major problem resulting from soil erosion is that when soils are carried away by water the sediment can be eventually deposited in streams, lakes, rivers, or the ocean. Increased sediment in these water environments can hurt the plants and animals that live in them. It can also pollute the water, making it unfit for humans to drink.

Farmers can do several things in order to reduce soil erosion. They can let a field lay fallow and allow natural processes to restore the land to its original state. They can identify land that erodes easily and choose not to farm it at all. They can also use different plowing techniques that help protect the land (these will be discussed in more detail in Chapter 8, which deals with conservation). The protection needed on each piece of land is unique to that land, based on the type of soil, the landscape, and the needs of the crops that are being planted.

The success of agriculture is closely tied to soil fertility and health. As illustrated in the previous chapter, the six principal resource cycles are critical for the management of nutrients between the soil, plants, air, and water. Agriculture can upset this delicate balance because it involves new land use controlled by humans. Because many crops have high nutrient demands, they can remove those nutrients from the soil faster than native plants would. When crops are harvested, the nutrients are removed and cannot be recycled into the ground as they would be in a natural system.

Crops also require large amounts of nitrogen and phosphorus in order to grow, which depletes these elements from the soil. When soils have a lower fertility, farmers must correct this imbalance by adding inorganic (chemical) or organic fertilizers to the soil. If runoff carries fertilizers away, this can contaminate streams, rivers, and lakes. All farmers must take these issues into consideration, whether they run large farms or small farms; farms that produce multiple commodities (goods) or only one; or single-family farms or company farms.

Some farms have a monoculture—they only grow one crop, such as wheat or cotton. This is a specialized production system that uses chemically managed row crops, which can result in soil erosion. This can also quickly use up certain nutrients from the soil that the crops need to grow and thereby lower the fertility of the soil.

A farmstead in Green County, Wisconsin. *(Courtesy of the U.S. Department of Agriculture; photo by Ron Nichols)*

Other farms have a mixed-crop environment, where they grow several different commodities that do well in their geographical region. Still other farms not only produce agricultural commodities but also raise livestock. Some farms, such as dairy farms, may specialize in raising livestock. In intensive livestock production, where animals are kept confined in pens, animal health and waste management are extremely important issues that must be dealt with. There is a strong moral and ethical debate about whether livestock should be confined in intensive production systems. Confining livestock is also an increasing source of surface water and groundwater pollution. Managing livestock waste can be very expensive. Each type of farm has its own management issues, depending on the type of farm it is.

TILLING METHODS

Because of the wide variation across the country in farming operations, commodities produced, and different environmental and climatic factors present, farming has evolved over the years. Traditionally, farmers have practiced a system of repeated plowing, **discing**, and cultivating to raise their crops. In the 1970s, however, because they were trying to control soil erosion, no-till and reduced-till farming methods began to be used along with traditional methods. The concept behind the no-till approach is to leave the soil alone. This approach uses chemicals instead of plowing and discing to enhance soil fertility. Because the soil structure is not disturbed, worm activity (nature's aerators) is able to leave the soil structure porous (with open spaces) so that nutrients can move down through the soil profile faster than they can using conventional tillage.

The reduced-till method is a combination of no-till and conventional plowing methods. Both require a substantial amount of chemical fertilizers and pesticides. Today, there is conventional farming and what many refer to as **alternative farming**. Alternative farming is a general term used to describe many different farming methods and philosophies.

CONVENTIONAL AGRICULTURE

Conventional farming is generally associated with large areas of land that require a lot of equipment and energy, and these farms are often expensive to operate. When they have livestock, conventional farms are usually associated with intensive animal-husbandry operations.

Conventional farming also uses new scientific approaches and new technology in order to maximize productivity and profits. These farms use large amounts of herbicides, pesticides, and artificial fertilizers. Conventional farming is a business whose goal is to maximize production.

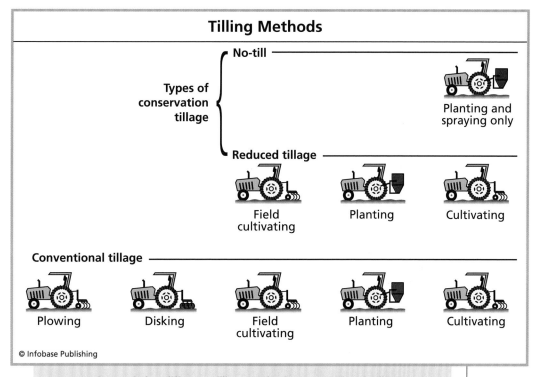

Tilling Methods

Types of conservation tillage

No-till — Planting and spraying only

Reduced tillage — Field cultivating | Planting | Cultivating

Conventional tillage — Plowing | Disking | Field cultivating | Planting | Cultivating

© Infobase Publishing

A comparison of the different tilling methods: conventional tillage versus conservation tillage methods (reduced tillage or no-till) is shown here. The conventional method introduces much more equipment and disruption to the surface of the field than the two conservation methods.

When a conventional farming site is set up, the land is developed, fenced in, and supplied with water. If the land will be used for agriculture, it is then cultivated and planted. If it is going to be used for livestock, it is cleared, re-brushed, and grazed. Standard types of agrochemicals (herbicides and pesticides) are used. The final step is to harvest the commodity.

Traditional farming has adapted to a wide variety of local conditions, has been able to successfully produce many different types of food reliably (year after year), has reduced problems from disease and insects, has used machinery and labor efficiently, and has been able to profit financially. Traditional farming provides food by using centuries of accumulated experience from farmers.

ALTERNATIVE AGRICULTURE

Alternative farming is a general term that represents many different practices and agricultural methods that all share similar goals. Alternative agriculture places more emphasis on conservation of the land and preserving resources.

Practices that are emphasized in alternative farming include building new topsoil (composting); using natural biological approaches instead of chemical pesticides for controlling insects; and conserving soil by rotating crops, letting unused vegetation recycle back into the ground, plowing the land relative to its needs, and reducing the amount of tilling of the soil. The different components of alternative agriculture are summarized below.

SUSTAINABLE AGRICULTURE

Sustainable agriculture looks at the farming cycle as a whole system and is a commonly used term when referring to alternative farming. This places an emphasis on working in harmony with entire ecological systems. As farmers see shifts take place in our ever-changing environment, their goal is to change their farming methods to be in harmony with the environment.

They also look at the system as a living thing with different needs for different areas within the farm. Instead of applying the same practices evenly over the entire farm, each area on the farm is assessed and treated according to its own needs.

Sustainable agriculture seeks to balance farm profit over the long term with needs for good soil and clean water, a safe and abundant food supply, and rural communities that are rewarding to live in. Farmers of sustainable agriculture look at agriculture and ecology together, and refer to it as *agroecology*. In traditional methods, soil scientists study soils, hydrologists study water, and agronomists study crops. Studying these different components separately, however, can result in a lack of understanding or appreciation of how the entire system fits and works together. In agroecology, the entire system (soil, water, sun, plants, air, animals, microorganisms, and people) is studied together.

Farmers who practice sustainable agriculture strive to understand the complex relationships among all parts of the agroecosystem. Sustainable agriculture practices include the following:

1. Using no chemicals, or very few chemicals, to reduce pest damage to crops.
2. Using fewer herbicides (weed killers).
3. Minimizing runoff in order to reduce soil erosion.
4. Testing the soils to determine which nutrients are available.
5. Rotating crops so that the land is not overused or depleted of critical nutrients. Crop rotation also reduces insects and weeds.
6. Minimizing soil erosion by using contour plowing (discussed in Chapter 8), cover crops to protect the soil, no-till methods, and perennial plants (plants that bloom each year without having to be reseeded).
7. Improving and protecting wildlife habitats.
8. Monitoring grazing practices so that the land is not abused and overgrazed.

Some people have argued that sustainable farming is not as productive and is more expensive than traditional farming. Others have said that, even if that is the case, they are willing to pay more. Others maintain that it does not represent lower productivity but instead builds on current agricultural achievements and can produce large crops without harming the land.

Regardless of what people have to say in favor of sustainable farming or not, it has become an important part of agriculture in the last few years. Many farmers and ranchers have chosen to use more conservative practices on their lands, and they see it as the future of a successful, long-term relationship with the ecosystem.

ORGANIC FARMING

Organic does not refer to the food itself but how the food is produced. Organic foods are produced without using any synthetic pesticides or fertilizers. They are also not given any ionizing radiation. Organic crops are grown on soil that has been chemical-free for at least four years. Organic farming is also meant to maintain the land and keep the surrounding ecosystems healthy. Organic livestock cannot be fed non-organic feed or given any type of growth hormone or antibiotic. Before a product can be labeled *organic*, however, a government-approved certifier must inspect it.

When properly managed, organic farming reduces or eliminates water pollution and helps conserve water and soil on farms. Today, organic farming represents only a small section of agriculture, but it has been growing over recent years. Because it does not require expensive chemicals, many developing countries are able to produce organic crops to export to other countries.

Most organic farmers strive to make the best use of land, animal, and plant interactions; preserve the natural nutrients; and enhance biodiversity. They practice soil and water conservation to keep erosion down. They use organic manure and mulch to improve soil structure. They also use natural pest controls, such as biological controls (using an insect's natural predators), as well as plants with pest-control properties. They rotate their crops to keep production and fertility higher.

HYDROPONIC AGRICULTURE

Hydroponics is usually defined as "the cultivation of plants in water." *Hydroponic* is a combination of two Greek words that mean "water working." Hydroponic agriculture started out using only water in which to grow crops, but it has evolved over the years. It now means "the cultivation of plants without soil," because crops can be grown in water, sand, peat moss, and even rock wool.

Hydroponics works because plants do not feed on the soil—they feed on the minerals contained in the soil. Hydroponics makes those same minerals that plants need to grow available to the plants directly through water or through other media (although water is the most commonly used medium, so peat moss and rock wool do not become overused and depleted).

Farmers all over the world are using hydroponic techniques. They are an attractive choice when farmers lack fertile farmland. Many people use hydroponics in their homes so that they can have fresh vegetables all year long. People also grow hydroponic crops at home if they do not have a yard, because hydroponic crops can be grown in small, confined places.

This "soil-free gardening" has several advantages for people who grow gardens out of their homes. For example, there are no weeds to pick; pests or diseases usually associated with soil do not exist; the plants grow faster and use less space (because the roots do not need to spread out in search of food and water); and the entire system can be automated with a timer.

For commercial farmers, hydroponics also has several advantages. Hydroponics does not require large areas of farmland; crops can be produced in greenhouses or even in desert sands; nutrients can be applied directly to the roots of the plants where they are needed; water can be reused; and water is conserved because there is less evaporation and runoff. This means that even deserts can be used to produce food using limited amounts of water.

HORTICULTURE

Horticulture is the science and art of growing fruits, vegetables, flowers, and ornamental plants. Horticulture is a smaller-scale version of large-scale arable farming. Horticulture can produce more specialized produce than traditional agriculture. In addition to fruits and vegetables, there are also flowers, plants, garden trees, shrubs, and turf. Turf is pregrown grass that is cut below the root line so that the roots and soil it grew in are left intact. The turf just needs to be laid

An example of the artistic beauty of a carefully hand-cultivated bonsai tree. *(Courtesy of the U.S. Department of Agriculture; photo by Eric Newman)*

down on cleared ground and watered. Turf can be used to make an instant backyard or soccer field.

Fruit orchards are well maintained. Trees are watched closely for signs of disease or other problems. Many specialty fruits are also grown, such as raspberries. Because the fruit is soft and delicate, it must be harvested by hand (handpicked). This is why specialty fruits, like raspberries, blackberries, grapes, strawberries, and blueberries, are more expensive than other fruits, like apples and oranges.

Horticulture crops require more labor than arable crops. They also use better soil. These crops are usually sold in markets close to where they were produced instead of being trucked across the country or shipped to other countries. Horticulture crops can be more expensive than large-scale commercially grown crops, but many people like them because they are often fresher.

There are several advantages to growing horticultural crops. One part of horticulture is the use of enclosed greenhouses for farming. These are buildings made of glass. As the sun warms up the outside air, its rays penetrate through the glass walls and ceiling, heating the air inside the greenhouse. The glass allows the plants to receive the sunlight they need to grow. The heat is trapped inside the greenhouse by the glass. Greenhouses are kept warm and humid (substantial moisture in the air) inside so the plants never freeze. The plants are also protected from the damaging and cooling effects of the wind. This is sometimes called *controlled environment agriculture.* One advantage of a greenhouse is that crops can be cultivated all year long—even during the winter—so food can be grown out of season.

Horticulture also includes nurseries where ornamental plants and flowers are grown. The art of growing flowers and ornamental plants is referred to as *floriculture.* Flower arrangements, common at special occasions, such as weddings, are grown in nurseries. Another common product is outdoor gardening and decorative flowers that are popular in yards during the summer, such as petunias, marigolds, pansies, and roses.

A horticultural art form that is becoming increasingly popular is *bonsai.* A bonsai is a small tree that has been dwarfed by pruning and trained over time into an artistic shape. Other horticultural crops include herbs, nuts, bamboo, mushrooms, sprouts, wheatgrass, asparagus, lettuce, and tomatoes.

URBAN AGRICULTURE

People usually associate agriculture and farming with rural areas, but today, an increasing amount of agricultural production in the United States originates from within metropolitan areas (cities).

This type of agriculture is called *urban agriculture*. In America, people are involved in growing food because they enjoy doing it—it is a rewarding activity for many. In developing countries, however, many people in villages and towns must grow their own food for survival.

Urban agriculture is the conversion of unused parcels of land in cities into sustainable food-production areas. Although urban agriculture will never be a solution for providing vast amounts of food, it is a viable branch of alternative farming. As a form of sustainable agriculture, urban agriculture is able to incorporate the same elements of sustainable farming already discussed—just on a much smaller scale. It commonly involves composting, water quality assessment, yard and landscaping management, and wildlife management. It also provides beautiful parks and botanical gardens for others to enjoy.

Urban agriculture can mean rooftop gardening, backyard gardening, hydroponics, and community gardening. Many city dwell-

Urban and Community Agriculture in Action

Residents of the Rosebud Lakota Reservation in South Dakota began a community gardening project in 2003. They were able to grow enough food for their families and neighbors and also participate in a gardener's market to sell their produce—the only fresh market for hundreds of miles. Farming in the area is a challenge due to poor soils and an average annual rainfall of only 12 inches (30.5 centimeters), but the reservation's community pulled together and made the program successful. The gardeners took pride in their new endeavor—it was a way to do something healthy for their families and community.

Source: Sustainable Agriculture Research and Education Program

ers look at urban agriculture as part of a sustainable food system for the future.

COMMUNITY-BASED FARMING

One form of alternative agriculture is community-based farming—or community-supported agriculture, called CSA. CSA consists of many participants in a local community working together to cultivate and care for an area of land, which will produce food for them to eat.

CSA first began in Europe and Japan and was developed as a way to have a different social and economic system. Farming practices like this also exist in Israel on kibbutz farms. CSA in America provides an opportunity for nonfarmers and farmers to join together to advance agriculture. Many people participate in CSA so that they can have a direct connection to their personal food supply and because they are concerned about the widespread use of pesticides in conventional agriculture. They also want to participate in a stewardship role for the land and its future.

Participants usually purchase their share of the harvest ahead of time. Then, as the crops are grown and cultivated, from late spring to early fall, the participants receive a supply of the crops that are grown, such as fruits, vegetables, and herbs. An organic farming approach is often used.

PRECISION AGRICULTURE

Precision agriculture is a newly emerging component of farming. With growing populations and increasing demands on the land, being productive and efficient is becoming more important. Cutting-edge positioning and information space technologies have now entered agriculture. Satellites and geographical spatial technology have taken a role recently in finding practical ways to help farmers become better and more efficient.

Farmers can now operate their farms—from planting to harvesting—by managing every square foot of the land according to the needs of that particular square foot. Precision agriculture uses space satellite data (a science called remote sensing), soil sampling, and information management tools to make agricultural production as efficient as possible.

Precision agriculture uses technologies, such as Global Positioning System (GPS), Geographic Information System (GIS), and airborne images, to help farmers manage their fields. These high-tech systems can analyze soil and landscape characteristics (what type of soil it is, how steep the land is, what direction the slope faces, and how much direct sunshine it receives). These high-tech systems can determine whether pests are present (by assessing insect damage) long before humans can see the results of an infestation because satellites can pick up wavelengths in the infrared region, which are the first wavelengths to reveal changes in plant health.

GPS can provide the farmer with specific information on tillage, planting, weeds, insect and disease infestations, cultivation, and irrigation. Machine control systems automate equipment to save time and costs that would normally have to be paid to a field operator. Laser-based tools provide information on land-leveling requirements and underground drainage. This equipment collects field data, which is then downloaded into computer systems and analyzed with special software to help the farmer determine the best farming practice for his land. These systems can help the farmer manage small areas of the farm differently—according to his or her needs.

A computer can be used to analyze all the spatial data that has been collected (such as soil types, crop yield, water drainage, rainfall, and chemical doses) and look at overall relationships between the different types of information that affect crop production in a specific place. For example, this type of analysis might indicate that the farmer needs to add more fertilizer to one field, more water to another field, or pesticides in still another area.

Precision agriculture allows farmers to improve the crops they grow, provides information for better farming practices, reduces unnecessary applications of pesticides or other chemicals, and gives farmers better data to manage their lands more effectively.

BIOTECHNOLOGY FOR PLANTS, ANIMALS, AND THE ENVIRONMENT

Along with the multitude of different farming options and techniques, another issue that affects farmers is biotechnology. As producing food efficiently becomes more critical, scientists and farmers have turned to the science of genetic engineering.

Modern biotechnology is a refinement of the breeding techniques that have been used by farmers to improve plants for thousands of years. Scientists have improved plants since the late 1800s by changing their genetic makeup. This has been accomplished through techniques such as crossbreeding and hybridization, where two related plants are cross-fertilized and the resulting offspring have characteristics of both parent plants.

Many foods already commonly available that are products of these techniques include hybrid maize, nectarines (genetically altered peaches), and tangelos (a hybrid of tangerine and grapefruit). Today, by inserting one or more genes into a plant, scientists can produce a plant with new, advantageous characteristics. Because of the increased precision offered by bioengineered methods, the risk of introducing negative traits is likely to be lessened.

Genetic engineering can be used to modify the genetic compositions of plants, animals, and microorganisms. Currently, technology is used mainly to modify crops. Genetically engineered products must go through a period of research and development before they can be used. Many products never make it past the research stage—they never get developed for use.

During the past decade, biotechnology has made available genetically engineered crops—corn, soybean, and cotton—that have been altered to control insects and weeds. Crops are being engineered to better tolerate the effects of herbicides, insects, and viruses. Food animals, such as engineered fish, are also being studied.

Biotechnology can also affect medicine and industry. Recently, corn has been engineered to produce pharmaceuticals (medicine and drugs) as well as industrial and research chemicals. Scientists are working on developing corn-based drugs and vaccines.

Some scientists are concerned that engineered products might be harmful to people's health or to the environment. Common concerns include the possibility that engineered crops might contaminate the food supply with drugs, kill beneficial insects along with harmful ones, cross-pollinate with wild species, or otherwise impact natural resources. Some worry that engineered fish could alter native ecosystems, even killing off native species. Other scientists disagree, saying that traits developed by modern biotechnology are more predictable and controllable than the hybrid methods used in the past and that we have a better understanding of the changes being made and are in a better position to understand safety issues.

Scientists are also experimenting with ways to delay the ripening of tomatoes. They are working on methods to increase dairy cows' milk production. Currently, a product called bovine growth hormone (BGH) is being used on about 10% of the dairy cows in the United States to achieve this goal. Plants and foods produced using biotechnology are put through strict testing procedures before being offered to the public.

In the future, scientists may find ways to engineer animals to produce leaner meat, engineer chickens and turkeys to resist avian diseases, and produce plants that are not vulnerable to insects. New developments and discoveries are being made all the time in this fast-paced branch of science and technology.

USE OF THE LAND AND AGRICULTURAL DIVERSITY

This chapter looks at various uses that affect farmland, such as irrigation methods, the use of pesticides and fertilizers, the role of tilling, and the progression of urban encroachment and the concept of conservation easements. Some exciting new uses of agriculture, mainly as new and innovative sources of energy and products that can help us now and in the future to supply valuable fuel and electricity, are also explored.

IRRIGATION

In addition to drinking water, irrigation—the use of water for agriculture (growing crops)—is one of the most important uses of water. Over half of the world's usable fresh water is used to irrigate crops. Large farms that produce huge surpluses of food must have access to large quantities of water. Water can come from rivers, lakes, reservoirs, and wells. Without irrigation water, it would be impossible for farmers to grow crops. Irrigation also offsets the effects of climate. Dry

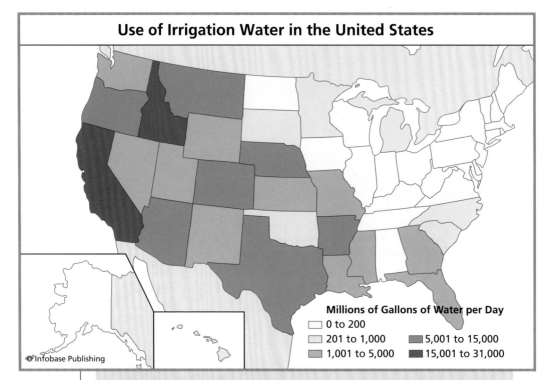

Use of Irrigation Water in the United States

Millions of Gallons of Water per Day

☐ 0 to 200
☐ 201 to 1,000   ▨ 5,001 to 15,000
▨ 1,001 to 5,000   ■ 15,001 to 31,000

©Infobase Publishing

Irrigation use in the United States during the year 2000. *(Source: United States Geological Survey)*

desert areas, such as in the American West, would never be able to farm without irrigation.

When water is used for irrigation, only half of it is reused by returning to the ground or back into a stream. The rest is lost through evaporation into the air or transpiration from plants, or it is lost before it reaches the field, such as from leaky water pipes.

In the western United States, where there is not a lot of rainfall—some areas may receive only 12 inches (30.5 centimeters) per year—water is a scarce and very valuable resource. When these dry areas experience periods of drought, water becomes even more important. Most of the irrigation in the United States occurs in the western states. Irrigation water use includes all the water artificially applied to farm and horticultural crops as well as water used to irrigate parks and golf courses. Irrigation has been

An example of a center-pivot irrigation system. *(Courtesy of the Natural Resources Conservation Service; photo by Tim McCabe)*

around for as long as humans have been growing crops. Irrigation first started using water from a bucket. In many developing areas of the world, pouring water on fields is still done today. Developed countries have created mechanized methods that are much more efficient. There are several types of irrigation methods: furrow (flood) irrigation, drip irrigation, and spray irrigation.

Furrow irrigation, also called *flood irrigation*, is a method where water is pumped to the fields and allowed to flow along the ground in pre-dug ditches, or furrows, among the crops. This method is easy and inexpensive. It is not very efficient, however. Only about half of the water ever reaches the plants. Farmers can improve the effectiveness of flood irrigation by making sure their fields are leveled, releasing water only at certain

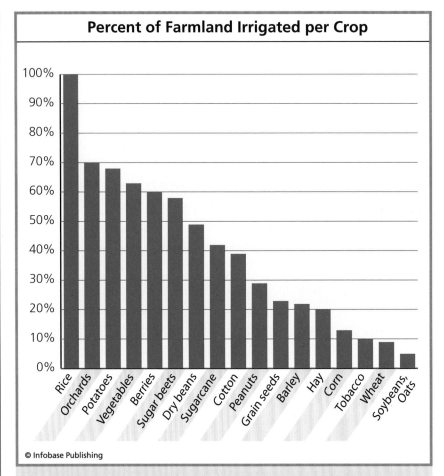

Percent of Farmland Irrigated per Crop

The amount of irrigation needed by crop type. (*Source: United States Geological Survey*)

© Infobase Publishing

intervals, and capturing runoff in ponds and pumping it back to the front of the field to be used again.

Drip irrigation is used for irrigating fruits and vegetables. Water is run through plastic pipes with holes in them that are either laid along the rows of crops or buried along the crops' root lines. This system is more efficient. Evaporation is reduced, and one-fourth of the water used is saved.

Spray irrigation is a method similar to watering a lawn with a hose. In agricultural applications, water flows through a long tube and is shot out by a system of spray guns. A common type is a center-pivot system. This system has a series of metal frames on rolling wheels that extend the water tube out into the fields. Electric motors move each frame in a big circle around the field—one end serves as the center and remains stationary while the line of sprayers scribes a circle around it. From above, the irrigated ground is in the shape of a perfect circle.

An even more efficient method of spray irrigation is a system where water is gently sprayed from a hanging pipe. This cuts down on water being evaporated or blown away before it even hits the ground in the dry, windy air of the western United States. According to the U.S. Geological Survey, this method increases irrigation efficiency from 60% (with traditional spray irrigation) to more than 90%.

Other issues that farmers pay close attention to are the avoidance of **leaching** and salinization. It is often a delicate balance between draining the soils to keep salts from collecting and harming the plants and having too much drainage, which carries essential nutrients away.

PESTICIDES

Pests do a lot of harm to plants. *Pest* is a general term applied to any undesirable plant, animal, or microbe. Agricultural pests are those that compete with or damage crops and livestock. Pests reduce the efficiency of farming because they not only harm the crop or livestock but are also expensive for the farmer to eliminate. Pesticides are used to control pests.

After World War II (1939–1945), complex chemical pesticides were developed, and pesticide use increased dramatically worldwide. Today, in the United States alone, 661 million pounds (almost 300 million kilograms) of pesticides are used per year. Pesticides include a large range of products, including bactericides (kills bacteria), insecticides (kills insects), fungicides (kills fungus), herbicides (kills weeds), and rodenticides (kills rodents).

There are also narrow-spectrum and broad-spectrum pesticides. A narrow-spectrum pesticide targets specific pest species. Broad-spectrum pesticides target a wider range of organisms, which can include pest species as well as some nonpest and beneficial species. Unfortunately, scientists have discovered that many pest species reproduce so fast that they can evolve and develop resistance to pesticides—a phenomenon called *pesticide resistance*. Because of this, pesticides continually need to be redeveloped in order to remain effective on the pests.

Another problem with pesticides is that they can have widespread environmental effects beyond impacting just those pests they were designed to fight. Sometimes, other insects are killed along with the pests—including insects that may naturally eat the targeted insect or valuable insects that are needed to pollinate plants.

Some pesticides are not environmentally friendly. If they do not biodegrade well, they can collect in the tissues of plants and animals, or collect in sediments and then reenter the food web. A practical example of a pesticide that causes problems like this is DDT. The insecticide DDT is a chlorinated hydrocarbon that was widely used in the United States until it was taken off the market in the 1970s.

DDT did not decompose, and if animals ate it, it remained in their tissues and was transferred through the food chain. Organisms at the top of the food chain and animals that lived a long time had the highest concentrations of DDT in their tissues. DDT caused a lot of damage in aquatic food chains and hurt pelicans, ospreys, and bald eagles. The DDT damaged their reproductive systems and caused them to produce thin, easily damaged eggshells. It caused their populations to significantly decline. Although it is no longer used in the United States, it is still used in the tropics to control mosquitoes.

One solution to using pesticides that damage the environment in large-scale settings is using integrated pest management (IPM) measures. IPM uses many possible solutions rather than just a single method of pest control (unlike pesticides). In integrated pest management, farmers use techniques such as crop rotation (changing what is grown in a field—pests of one crop may not be pests of another crop); selecting resistant varieties (some plants are more resistant to pests); mechanical cultivation; changing planting and harvesting times; biological control (using other living organisms to control pests—a predator that controls

An example of an airborne application of pesticides in a field. The airplane flies very low to the ground to avoid wasting the chemical in the wind. *(Courtesy of the U.S. Department of Agriculture; photo by Tim McCabe)*

them naturally); and chemical control. If a chemical control (pesticide) is used at all, it is used sparingly after determining (1) what the specific pest causing the problem is and (2) how much and how often to apply the chemical for that particular pest.

FERTILIZERS

As plants grow, they naturally use the nutrients in the soil around them. When a plant dies, if it is left in place, it will start to decompose over time and its leaves and stems will rot. This natural process allows the nutrients from the plant to return to the soil, providing the soil with nutrients.

As seen in the resource cycles in Chapter 3, recycling of nutrients is important in order to keep soil healthy and productive. In agriculture, however, this critical cycle gets disturbed because, once the plant is grown, it is harvested as food instead of left in the ground to rot. When it is harvested, the nutrients go with the plant. Over time, this upsets the balance because the plants are using nutrients from the soil without replacing them. This makes the soil less fertile.

Plants must have a continuous supply of nutrients in order to grow well. When the soil's nutrients are depleted, the next planting of crops has fewer nutrients to draw from. This hurts the next crop, making it much less productive. Because of this imbalance created by harvesting the crops, farmers must add nutrients back into the soil in order to make it more fertile. The nutrients that are added are called *fertilizer*. When a crop has the nutrients it needs, it is healthier and more resistant to potential threats from temperature extremes, strong winds, birds and other animals, weeds, pests, and diseases. Adding nutrients to the soil is also important because some of the nutrients contained in the soil are either not in a form that the crops can use, or the nutrients cannot be supplied as fast as the crops need them. Fertilizers added to the soil keep crops at the peak of their performance.

There are two main types of fertilizers: organic and chemical. Organic fertilizers come from the remains of plants and animals. They usually act more slowly than chemical fertilizers, and they must be added in greater amounts. They also release the fertilizing elements when the soil is a certain temperature, making them more unpredictable than chemical sources.

One advantage of using organic fertilizer, however, is that organic nutrients are returned to the soil. Organic nutrients are important for the long-term health of the soil. Their presence in the topsoil acts like a sponge—holding air, water, and nutrients for plants to use. Examples of organic fertilizers include bonemeal, cottonseed meal, seaweed extract, legumes, manure (from horses, cows, pigs, chicken, or sheep), and green manure. Green manure is a cover crop that is grown and dug back into the soil. Green manure not only adds organic nutrients but also improves the physical structure of the soil. Examples of green manure are ryegrass, crimson clover, rough pea, horse bean, and common vetch.

Chemical fertilizers—also called synthetic fertilizers—are made up of mixtures of chemicals. Because different crops have different needs, chemical fertilizers can be tailored to specific types of crops. Chemical fertilizers consist of nitrogen, potassium (potash), and phosphate.

There are many methods of adding fertilizer to the soil. Green manure is planted; animal manure is applied with a spreader; and chemical fertilizers can be powders or liquids that are mixed up and sprayed.

TILLING

Tilling the soil before planting a crop is necessary for two reasons: to mix soil amendments (such as compost and fertilizer) into the soil, and to prepare the ground for planting. Because plowing disturbs the soil, which is disadvantageous, American farmers have developed methods of plowing that disturb the soil as little as possible. When soil is not disturbed, it is easier for the soil to contribute to the critical resource cycles (such as nitrogen, carbon, and phosphorus) that ensure healthy agriculture and livestock.

Reduced tillage, or conservation tillage, is the method that least disturbs the soil. When tilling is done using conventional methods—such as the moldboard plow—the top 8 inches (20.3 centimeters) of the soil is completely turned over, which buries crop residue and leaves the soil loose and prone to erosion. Reduced tillage, as explored in Chapter 4, leaves crop residue on the surface of the ground to cover and protect it from wind and rain. Farmers can use a no-till, mulch-till, or ridge till method to accomplish this. Tillage usually takes place in the fall and spring. Fall tilling is done to loosen up the soil that was compacted during the growing season and to mix remaining plant residues with the soil. Spring tilling readies the field for planting.

URBAN ENCROACHMENT

Over time, a common trend across the country has been the spread of urban areas. As urban areas grow, they encroach on agricultural land in many places. Because the land surface of the Earth is a fixed resource, there is only a certain amount of it that is available for agriculture. Many

An example of urban encroachment in Richmond, Virginia. *(Courtesy of the U.S. Department of Agriculture; photo by Tim McCabe)*

people are concerned that, as agricultural land is converted to urban uses, having less agricultural land available may spell disaster for a world experiencing rapid rates of population growth and urbanization.

To increase the productivity of the land that is available for agriculture, it must be used in a more sustainable and efficient manner. One way that scientists help farmers estimate the productivity of their land is by using satellite images to inventory agricultural use and efficiency. Satellites record the agricultural land, enabling scientists to record farmland. Satellites can differentiate between crop types, determine soil moisture levels, and calculate overall biomass density and plant health. This information can be combined with other information—such as farming practices and soil conditions—to create future crop-yield predictions. This is a valuable tool for markets as well as decision makers in charge of food security.

An example of using high-tech resources is precision farming, mentioned in Chapter 4. The data collected from space can provide farmers with important information to help them manage their farms more effectively. Farmers realize they must manage their land more efficiently, as more and more acres of land each year are lost to urban encroachment. Fortunately, as farmers have gained insight over the years into increasing productivity and also taking better care of their land, it has been possible to produce greater amounts of food per acre.

Another way farmers are protecting the future of agricultural land is through agricultural conservation easements. A conservation easement is a practical protection tool that can directly benefit farmers and ranchers, as well as their land, and provide for the future of agriculture. A conservation easement is a method to slow the loss of open space. It is a development restriction that a person puts on his or her land. In this way, the landowner voluntarily protects the future of the land by limiting it to agricultural and open space uses only. It keeps subdivisions from being built or any other development that would damage the agricultural value or productivity of the land. In return, the landowner receives tax benefits. This keeps agricultural land in active production by removing development pressures.

This is one method that farmers can use to make sure that future generations will have productive farmland and that land stewardship will be set in place for sustainable agriculture. It also provides other benefits for the land, such as scenic and habitat values. Conservation easements have become important to many states in the western United States, such as California, Utah, and Colorado.

EXPERIMENTAL FARMING: USES OF OTHER FARM PRODUCTS

There are more benefits from farming and ranching than food production. Many scientists today are trying to find new sources of energy and fuel to offset the demand for energy and the high costs of fossil fuels. In the past decade, there have been significant advances in the production of what scientists call *biofuels*—fuels made from biological materials.

Biomass

Biomass is any organic material that does not come from fossil fuels and can be converted to a fuel and used to generate electricity. Biomass can be waste products or crops planted for the purpose of producing energy. These crops are called *dedicated crops*.

Biomass generates electricity through the process of combustion, which releases the stored solar energy that is contained in plant matter. It is becoming an attractive source of renewable energy because, unlike solar or wind energy, biomass can be used at any time—it does not have periods of selective availability (solar power can only be generated when the sun is shining; and wind power, when the wind is blowing). This is important because it means electricity can be generated when it is needed the most.

Biomass for a power plant—also called *feedstocks*—can come in many different forms:

1. Wood residues: This is wood left over from other uses. For example, from unused wood in lumber mills, urban tree trimmings, unused residential construction material, demolition material, forest thinning, wood pallets, or anything else made of wood that is not being used.
2. Animal waste: Dry animal waste—usually from chickens and turkeys—can be burned directly for heat and power. Wet manure can be used to produce biogas.
3. Agricultural residues: These are crop components left after processing has been completed, such as oat hulls, nut hulls, and sugarcane. They can also be residue left in a field after harvesting, such as wheat straw.
4. Energy crops: These are crops dedicated to the sole production of energy. These include wood from willows, poplars, sycamore, and maple. Prairie grass is another type of energy crop.
5. Biofuels: These are liquid fuels that are used mainly as fuel for trucks and other forms of transportation. They include ethanol and biodiesel.

Sources of Biomass

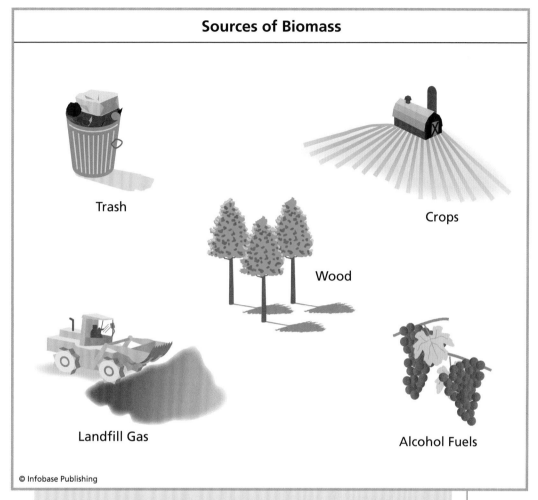

Trash

Crops

Wood

Landfill Gas

Alcohol Fuels

© Infobase Publishing

Biomass is organic material that can be used as a renewable source of energy.

In order to use biomass to produce energy, it must go through a preparation process called *homogenization*. Homogenization converts all the particles—which are usually different sizes—to uniformly sized particles. This is accomplished through a process of sorting materials by size class, and then cutting, grinding, or pulverizing them. Electricity from biomass is generated in a similar way to coal-fired electricity. Sometimes, biomass is used along with coal in a power production plant. Using biomass and coal together to produce energy is called cofiring. There are several cofiring experimental plants around the country, such as in Iowa and Wisconsin.

Gasification is another process being experimented with as a future source of energy generation. Gasification involves heating the biomass to high temperatures in the absence of oxygen, which causes the volatile (readily vaporizable at a relatively low temperature) portion of biomass to gasify. Nearly 80% of the biomass is volatile. The remaining biomass can then be gasified through a steam injection process. The gas can be used in efficient, low-polluting combustion turbines, similar to those used for natural gas or fuel cells. Although gasification is still an emerging technology, it has the potential to become an important component for electricity generation in the future.

Biomass as a renewable energy source does have environmental impacts—some positive and some negative. The combustion of biomass can produce the same air pollutants as fossil fuel combustion. Depending on the type of generator and emission-control technology that is used, however, pollutants can be kept at a level lower than those generated from burning fossil fuel.

Advantages of biomass include the fact that it does not contribute to global (greenhouse) warming like fossil fuels do. This is because the carbon dioxide that is released when the biomass is burned is offset by the carbon dioxide that was initially consumed through photosynthesis when the crop was growing. Biomass can also reduce soil erosion, improve water quality near streams, and provide habitat for wildlife.

As biomass technology advances, it is becoming more affordable and attractive as an alternative energy resource. It is already affordable to industries that produce biomass as waste products, such as wood-paper product factories like paper mills. As the technology advances and it becomes less expensive, biomass promises to be a valuable energy resource.

Biogas Digesters

Biogas digesters are of extreme interest to scientists because they can turn organic wastes from farms, factories, and cities into a source of renewable energy. Biogas digesters are treatment systems similar to those used by sewage treatment plants. There are three main types used on farms:

1. Covered lagoon—the lagoon is covered with an impermeable surface and is a common system for liquid manure.
2. Complete mix digester—this works with manure that is partially solid. The manure is processed in a heated tank, and the solids are kept in suspension by a mixer.
3. Plug-flow digester—this is used for cow manure. It mixes the manure and moves it through the digester in clumps (called plugs). Biogas is created and stored under an impermeable cover.

Biogas digesters work on the same principle as anaerobic digestion, which is a natural, biological process similar to composting that breaks down liquid manure and other organic wastes. It produces biogas that is about 55% to 70% methane, the primary component of natural gas. *Anaerobic* means "without oxygen." Therefore, the bacteria that produce biogas can only survive if they are not exposed to oxygen in the air.

There are several environmental benefits to the anaerobic digestion that produces biogas. Without oxygen, odors are reduced. Biogas is a renewable resource—referred to as **green energy production**. The digestion process reduces harmful pathogens (a specific causative agent of disease). It also reduces greenhouse gasses because methane, which is a powerful greenhouse gas (23 times more powerful than carbon dioxide, the most common greenhouse gas), is captured and burned in anaerobic digestion, so it does not get released into the atmosphere.

There are some environmental concerns, however, for on-farm digesters. Nitrogen and ammonia emissions can pollute the air if effective management processes, such as maintaining a crust on the storage pond, are not followed. Another concern is water pollution from potential surface water runoff or groundwater contamination from leakage. There are also air emissions from burning biogas—although they are significantly cleaner than existing coal-fired power plants. Digesters are seen as

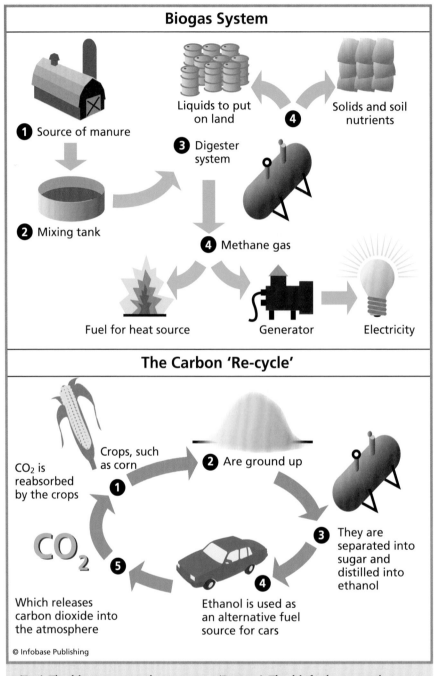

Biogas System

1 Source of manure

2 Mixing tank

3 Digester system

Liquids to put on land

4

Solids and soil nutrients

4 Methane gas

Fuel for heat source

Generator

Electricity

The Carbon 'Re-cycle'

CO_2 is reabsorbed by the crops

1

Crops, such as corn

2 Are ground up

3 They are separated into sugar and distilled into ethanol

4 Ethanol is used as an alternative fuel source for cars

5 Which releases carbon dioxide into the atmosphere

CO_2

© Infobase Publishing

(Top) The biogas generation process; (Bottom) The biofuels generation process of ethanol and the recycling of carbon.

a useful source of energy, but scientists do not see them ever becoming a primary energy source that can replace fossil fuels. Instead, they are likely to remain a supplemental form of alternative energy.

Biofuels

The past few years have seen tremendous growth in the use of biofuels to replace petroleum-based transportation fuels. Biofuels include ethanol, biodiesel, and alfalfa products.

Ethanol production has grown significantly. Current U.S. production is approximately 3 billion gallons (about 11.3 billion liters) of ethanol per year for use in cars and trucks. Many farmers own the ethanol-producing plants. Ethanol is a clean-burning, renewable product made from fermented agricultural products such as corn. Because ethanol contains oxygen, it provides a cleaner and more-efficient fuel than fossil fuel. When it is used in vehicles, it reduces carbon dioxide (a major contributor to global warming). Although ethanol does release some carbon dioxide when it is burned, the crops that produce ethanol recycle it. Many scientists believe it creates a greenhouse cycle where the gasses are used again by plants instead of remaining in the atmosphere.

In addition to corn, other crops are being experimented with as a source of ethanol in order to increase efficiency. Methods to convert cellulose (the fibrous matter in plants) into ethanol show the most promise for the future. **Perennial crops**, such as switch grass, are also candidates for the production of ethanol.

Biodiesel is a vegetable-based alternative to petroleum for diesel engines. It is a high-performance fuel that can be used in all diesel engines to significantly reduce harmful emissions. It is made from 80% to 90% vegetable oil and 10% to 20% alcohol. Biodiesel is a fuel produced from a chemical reaction between soybean oil, methanol, and lye. Waste grease (cooking oil) from cooking food can be used in place of soybean oil. Many restaurants contribute their used cooking oil to be converted into biodiesel. It can be used in its pure form or can be blended with petroleum diesel. Any percentage of biodiesel can be used, but 2% and 20% are the most common.

Biodiesel as a transportation fuel is becoming more common. It can also be used in emergency and remote diesel electric generators. An advantage of using biodiesel blended with petroleum diesel for backup power generation is that it reduces some of the harmful air emissions that are generated from petroleum diesel generators alone. Biodiesel can be used in all diesel equipment.

Over the past five years, the price of biodiesel has dropped, but it is still rather expensive compared to other fuels. Like ethanol, biodiesel also results in a net reduction in greenhouse gases. It is also completely biodegradable; less toxic than table salt; and less combustible, which makes it easier to handle, store, and transport. Biodiesel also lubricates the engine so it will last longer. In addition, it helps keep fuel lines, injectors, and combustion chambers clean.

Researchers are currently working with genetically engineered alfalfa to produce industrial enzymes. Enzymes are proteins that modify chemical reactions. They are used in many diverse industries and products, such as animal feeds, paper processing, and laundry detergent. One of the primary advantages of using alfalfa for producing industrial enzymes is that all of the residue left over after the enzymes have been extracted can be used for animal feed or even to produce electricity. Some researchers also believe that alfalfa enzymes may be useful for biopulping in the paper industry and toxic waste cleanup.

Currently, the USDA is experimenting with converting alfalfa into several different products. The leaves are being tested for use as raw, biodegradable plastic beads, industrial products, and better livestock feed. The alfalfa stems are being used in the production of ethanol.

In addition to plastics and fuel, alfalfa may be a renewable resource for replacing other petroleum-based products and nonrenewable resources, such as nitrogen and phosphorus fertilizers. This would be important in preventing fertilizers from polluting water. There are several advantages to using alfalfa. It can be harvested several times each growing season and needs replanting only every four to six years. Alfalfa also replenishes the soil with nutrients and is easy to grow. As science progresses and technology improves, inexpensive and new sources of energy like these will continue to be developed.

THE ROLE OF THE CENSUS IN PLANNING FOR FUTURE LAND USE

The National Agricultural Statistics Service (NASS), operated by the USDA, is important not only for conducting the agricultural census and providing information to farmers on fair crop prices, but for providing other data as well. The data it provides is used in agribusiness to develop market strategies and determine the most effective locations for service to agricultural producers. Farm organizations use data from NASS to evaluate and propose programs and policies that help agricultural producers. This allows efforts like biofuels and other uses of farmland to be addressed and facilities to be located for the most efficient experimentation and production. The data provided by NASS can also be used to forecast future energy needs for agricultural producers and their communities. Colleges and universities use the data in their research programs—such as those involving biofuels—to develop new and improved methods to enhance agricultural production.

THE IMPORTANCE OF AGRICULTURE

There is such a convenient and plentiful supply of food in the United States that sometimes it is easy to forget the important role that agriculture plays in our lives every day. Each time someone has a bowl of cereal for breakfast, a hamburger and fries for lunch, or puts on a new pair of jeans or hiking boots, agriculture has had an effect on our lives.

Agriculture plays an extremely important role in what people eat, what they wear, and where they live. It affects not only people in the United States, but everyone in the world.

This chapter examines the importance of the goods and services humans receive from agriculture; how agricultural products get from the farm to the plate; the effect shortages and surpluses have on our lives; how agriculture is traded globally; programs in place by governments to help combat world hunger; and, finally, how even people who live in cities can have a taste of rural life.

GOODS AND SERVICES

Many goods and services result from agriculture, including both tangible and intangible varieties. Tangible goods are items that can be picked up and physically felt. These are the items people trade, buy, and sell. Tangible agricultural goods include fruits; vegetables; grains; meat; dairy products; fabric made from cotton or wool; and leather used for shoes, purses, upholstery, and furniture.

Tangible services create employment opportunities in many types of businesses. The agriculture trade supplies jobs not only in the growing and harvesting of crops or the raising of livestock, but also in the manufacturing and operation of transportation and equipment. This includes the manufacture of farm equipment (tractors, tillers, seed drills, hay balers, and combines); equipment to transport the raw goods to be processed and marketed (trucks and trailers); industries that process and preserve the goods, such as canneries and packagers; and transportation to ship the processed goods nationally and internationally (trucks, trains, ships, and planes). It provides for the tangible goods and services of supermarkets and other dealers that sell and market agricultural products. It provides jobs for those who manufacture clothing, furniture, blankets, and other items made from fiber, as well as those who sell the items in local stores for customers to purchase. There are also intangible goods and services associated with agriculture. These are the more abstract benefits that people often neglect to think about. Intangible items include clear-flowing streams and safe drinking water (when proper farm management practices are used). Unpolluted streams and water sources also benefit wildlife and support biodiversity. Agriculture also contributes to the creation and maintenance of scenic landscapes.

AGRIBUSINESS

Agriculture is a business in many parts of the world. In areas of subsistence farming—where a family farms to produce goods for their own needs, without much excess—agriculture does not serve as a business, but a method of sustenance and survival. This is common in many of the poor, or developing, areas of the world. Nearly 40% of the world's population and about two-thirds of the world's farmers live under these conditions.

Commercial farming systems, on the other hand, produce agricultural commodities for sale. The money made from sales is partially used to purchase items, such as tractors and machinery, fertilizers, pesticides, improved plants, better breeds of animals, and other technological innovations. These types of farms are usually large because they are expensive to operate. These farming systems are found in the tropical and subtropical plantations that grow bananas and sugarcane and in the midlatitudes, such as in North America.

Some countries grow cash crops. These are crops that are in high demand and can be grown in large quantities in specific areas of the world. For example, sugar needs a hot, damp climate; coffee needs a hot climate, rainfall, and higher mountain elevations. Tea needs to grow on hillsides in rainy areas. Bananas grow well in tropical environments. Because there is a worldwide demand for specific items such as these, the farmers in tropical countries grow as much of these commodities as they can. These cash crops are sold all around the world and bring in a lot of money, but there are risks to specializing in just one commodity for trade. If these farmers grow too much of a particular cash crop, that creates more supply than demand, which drops the price of the commodity. If the climate is bad, and the cash crop does not grow well one year, that hurts the country selling it because that crop may be the only one the country provides in large enough quantities to make a living from.

A total of 7.8 billion acres of land in the world is potentially arable. Of that, only 3.5 billion acres (not even half) is actually used to grow crops. The reason for so much unused potential agricultural land is that it is in areas that do not have the transportation or other **infrastructure** needed to support commercial food production. For example, in order to run a business in agriculture, there need to be roads and railroads available to transport the goods and processing plants where the goods can go to be prepared for sale (canneries, slaughterhouses, and packing plants). Many countries lack roads or the train routes necessary to move goods to and from agricultural production areas.

Almost all the nutrients humans need in order to survive come from three sources: crops; animal products (meat, milk, eggs); and aquatic foods (seafood). Among crops, the cereals (wheat, rice, corn, and millet) occupy three-fourths of the cropland area and provide about three-fourths of the world's intake of calories.

There are also trackable trends in items used for food consumption. In the past 25 years, studies show that Americans have been eating more fruits and vegetables, fish, flour and cereal products, poultry, carbonated drinks, and cheese. There has been a slight decline in the consumption of red meat, eggs, milk, and coffee.

Those involved in agribusiness must keep up with the trends in agricultural consumption in order to adequately provide the goods the public wants. Lifestyle trends over time have a notable impact. For example, convenient prepackaged meals are in higher demand today to accommodate busy lifestyles than they were 25 years ago. Fast foods have contributed to the increase of greater consumption of cooking oils in fried food.

Scientists have determined that the average American today consumes more food, more snacks, bigger portions, and more calories than in the 1970s. More calories, along with reductions in average physical activity are behind an increase in obesity among adults, adolescents, and children in the United States. This is becoming an alarming trend to nutritionists and those involved in health care.

These issues are also considered in agribusiness. In order for farmers to produce what is in demand, they must carefully monitor market trends—producing too much of what the public does not want is as harmful to business as not producing enough of what the public demands. Agribusinesses use the census data provided by the USDA's National Agricultural Statistics Service. The data is used to develop market strategies and to determine the most effective locations for service to agricultural producers. Farm organizations use it to develop programs and policies that can help agricultural producers. Rural electric companies use this data to forecast future energy needs for agricultural producers and their communities.

HOW PRODUCTS GET FROM THE FARM TO THE PLATE

Once a farmer produces a commodity, whether it is fruits, vegetables, grains, meat, or dairy products, it does not go directly to the grocery store to be sold. It must be harvested and transported to facilities where it is processed. Grains can be stored in silos for use later, but fresh food does not last very long. It can dry up, lose its nutrients, or rot. Many foods are only harvested once a year, even though the demand for foods exists all year long. Some commodities must travel great distances—such as bananas from the tropics to the United States.

When foods are processed, they can go through different types of preservation processes. They can be canned, which allows them to last a year or more. Food can also be processed and frozen. This includes meats, fish, dairy products, fruits, and vegetables. Food can also be dried or preserved with agents such as salt or sugar.

When some foods are processed, they are irradiated as a method of food preservation. Food irradiation provides the same benefits as processing by heat, refrigeration, or freezing; or when it is treated with chemicals to destroy insects or bacteria that cause food to spoil or that make people sick. Irradiation also makes it possible to keep food longer and in better condition in warehouses and people's homes. Until recently, only irradiated dried spices and enzymes were marketed in the United States, although other countries, such as Belgium, the Netherlands, and France, use irradiation to preserve large amounts of food.

The process uses ionizing radiation. This is short wavelengths of light that have the ability to destroy microorganisms that cause food to spoil (X-rays are also a form of shorter wavelengths of light). For example, strawberries that have been irradiated will last two to three weeks in the refrigerator instead of only a few days like they normally would without irradiation.

Although irradiation is used in about 36 countries worldwide, in the United States, its use has remained limited because many people fear that it may be harmful to our health. The Food and Drug Administration (FDA), however, has approved irradiation for eliminating insects from wheat, potatoes, flour, spices, tea, fruits, and vegetables. Irradiation can be used to control sprouting and ripening. It is used on pork to control a disease called trichinosis and on poultry to control a food poisoning caused by bacteria called salmonella. The following table summarizes foods that can be irradiated and the reasons for irradiating them.

Irradiation has many potential uses. It can be used to treat large quantities of potatoes kept in bulk storage in warehouses so they do not sprout during their stay. Scientists are also looking at ways that irradiation can be used in space flight. Irradiation is most useful for the following:

- Food preservation
- Sterilization
- Control of sprouting, ripening, and insect damage
- Control of food-borne illness

Ionizing Radiation and Food

Food	Reason to Irradiate
Grain, fruit	Keeps them from drying out; controls insects
Bananas, mangos, papayas, and other noncitrus fruits	Delays the ripening processing
Perishable foods	Delays spoiling and growing of mold
Meat poultry	Destroys disease-carrying organisms (salmonella, trichinae)

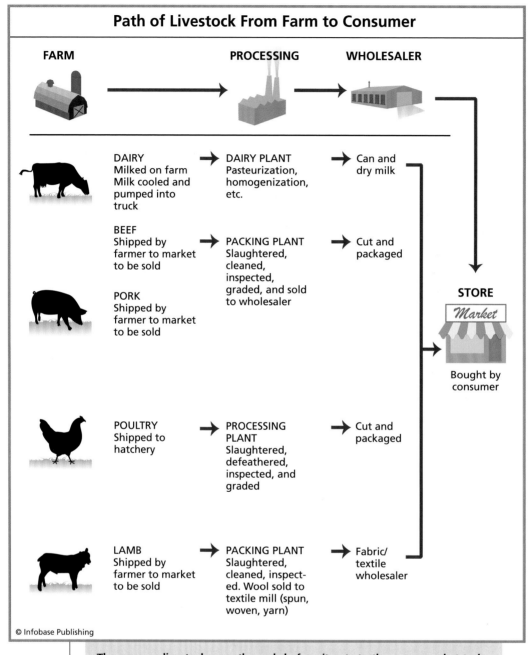

Path of Livestock From Farm to Consumer

FARM   **PROCESSING**   **WHOLESALER**

DAIRY
Milked on farm
Milk cooled and
pumped into
truck

→ **DAIRY PLANT**
Pasteurization,
homogenization,
etc.

→ Can and
dry milk

BEEF
Shipped by
farmer to market
to be sold

→ **PACKING PLANT**
Slaughtered,
cleaned,
inspected,
graded, and sold
to wholesaler

→ Cut and
packaged

PORK
Shipped by
farmer to market
to be sold

STORE

Market

Bought by
consumer

POULTRY
Shipped to
hatchery

→ **PROCESSING
PLANT**
Slaughtered,
defeathered,
inspected, and
graded

→ Cut and
packaged

LAMB
Shipped by
farmer to market
to be sold

→ **PACKING PLANT**
Slaughtered,
cleaned, inspect-
ed. Wool sold to
textile mill (spun,
woven, yarn)

→ Fabric/
textile
wholesaler

© Infobase Publishing

The process livestock goes through before it gets to the supermarket to be purchased by the consumer is shown above. *(Source: U.S. Department of Agriculture)*

The food that is irradiated in the United States is strictly regulated, inspected, and monitored by the FDA.

When livestock is sold for market, it must first be shipped by the farmer to a processing plant (slaughterhouse). Livestock, such as cows, sheep, poultry (chickens and turkeys), and pigs, are transported in large, ventilated trailers. At the packing or processing plant, the animals are slaughtered, inspected, graded, and sold to a wholesaler. The wholesaler then ships the meat to a processing plant that cuts and packages the meat for sale in grocery stores. The local grocery stores, or grocery chains, buy the meat from the wholesalers, where it is then bought by the consumer.

Livestock that produce dairy products (dairy cows, goats) are milked on the farm. The milk is cooled and then pumped into large container trucks. The raw milk is shipped to a dairy plant, where the milk is pasteurized, homogenized, and processed into other dairy products, such as butter, yogurt, and cheese. The dairy plant sells its products to a wholesaler, who sells them to the supermarket.

When the wool from sheep is processed, the wool is first sheared at the packing plant. It is then shipped to a textile mill, where it is spun, woven as fabric, or sold as yarn.

In addition to transporting and processing, commodities must also go through inspections to protect the customer against disease. Domestic food as well as imported foreign food must go through strict inspection procedures and meet certain requirements. Several events occurred to create the inspection requirements employed today.

When the U.S. Public Health Service began investigating the sanitary quality of milk in 1896, and epidemiological studies (studies that deal with the incidence, distribution, and control of disease in a population) showed a connection between raw milk consumption and human diseases, the Grade A Pasteurized Milk Ordinance (PMO) was established. The PMO is periodically revised and sets up specific guidelines that must be followed in heating milk, in order to destroy pathogens (agents of disease, such as viruses or bacteria) associated with milk.

In 1906, the Federal Meat Inspection Act addressed the issue of animal diseases that contaminated meat intended for human consumption. Meat processing and packing plants are now inspected for the presence of salmonella—pathogens that occur on raw meat and poultry products. The Food and Drugs Act of 1906 addressed food that had been corrupted, made impure, or fraudulently marketed by replacing more valuable with less valuable ingredients. In the early 1900s, regulations were put in place that required canneries to ensure the sterility of their products, so that people did not get sick from *Clostridium botulinum* (the bacteria that causes botulism or food poisoning).

Food safety criteria have evolved over time in the United States. In 1925, with the development of microbiological detection techniques for *E. coli*, the surgeon general established a conference of health officials. Later, the Environmental Protection Agency (EPA) was established, and microbiological as well as chemical hazards in drinking water contributed to the Safe Drinking Water Act of 1974. The EPA has enforced uniform, nationwide minimum drinking water standards for viruses, bacteria, and giardia.

Microbiological contaminants can enter the food chain at any point—from the farm to our plates. Because of this, responsibility for food safety resides with individuals at each point throughout the food process—from farmers, to manufacturers, to retail and food service professionals, to transportation and distribution professionals, to the consumer.

The USDA has established several services to protect the consumer:

- Animal and Plant Health Inspection Service (APHIS): It is responsible for regulating the import and export of plants and animals and some agricultural products. APHIS provides the nation with safe and affordable food.
- Food Safety Inspection Service (FSIS): It is responsible for ensuring that meat and poultry products are safe and accurately labeled.

As part of the APHIS food inspection procedure, a specially trained dog searches for the presence of fruit and drugs. *(Courtesy of the U.S. Department of Agriculture; photo by Ken Hammond)*

- Grain Inspection Packers and Stockyards Administration (GIPSA): It facilitates the movement of U.S. grain into the marketplace by providing farmers, grain handlers, processors, exporters, and international buyers with information about the quality of the grain being bought and sold.
- Federal Grain Inspection Service (FGIS): It establishes standards for grain, oilseeds, and other products for use in the country as well as those exported to other countries. It also monitors grain-handling practices.

Food is being processed for marketing in Albuquerque, New Mexico. *(Courtesy of the U.S. Department of Agriculture; Photo by Ken Hammond)*

These agencies function to ensure the safety of the American food supply. The United States government has instituted several laws and procedures to ensure food safety. In addition to strict regulations, food safety is also safeguarded through practices such as inspections and random sampling. The food safety standards that apply to foods produced in the United States also apply to foreign foods imported into the United States.

In the United States, food labels must contain specific information so that consumers understand what they are buying. Such information includes the following:

- The name of the product
- The net quantity of the contents
- The ingredients
- Information about additives and colors
- Nutrition information

The Environmental Protection Agency (EPA) establishes tolerances for pesticides, herbicides, and fungicides used in the fumigation of agricultural products. APHIS regulates the importation of animals that enter the country. Imports of livestock and poultry from other countries are quarantined for observation. Meat and poultry products can only be imported from countries approved by the United States.

APHIS also inspects and samples seeds imported from foreign countries to make sure that they are accurately labeled and free of noxious weeds. This agency ensures that the seeds, plants, bulbs, timber, flowers, vegetables, and fruits that are imported are healthy and do not pose a risk to our agriculture and natural resources. After completing all these processes, food is shipped to market for sale.

FOOD SHORTAGES AND SURPLUS

Even though there is more than enough food available to feed everyone in the world, many people do not have enough to eat. Every year, 12 million to 20 million people die from being undernourished or malnourished and from starvation and diseases that result from a lack of food. These problems are caused by factors such as food quantity, food quality, inadequate storage capabilities, inadequate food distribution, and poverty.

Food is grown differently in rich and poor nations. The developed countries, such as the United States, use industrialized methods of food production. The undeveloped countries do not have these advantages. They must rely more on the natural quality of the land and use intensive hand labor to farm. Science has also played an important role in increasing productivity in the developed world. Industrialized countries have learned many ways to increase food output, such as using fertilizers and pesticides, and creating hybrid crops.

This silo used for grain storage is in Charleston, South Carolina. Trucks filled with grain line up for inspection and unloading at the grain elevator. *(Courtesy of the U.S. Department of Agriculture; photo by Ken Hammond)*

Natural factors also affect the ability to develop productive farming. Climate plays a huge role in what can be grown. In addition, fluctuations in climate, such as years in which it is too dry or too wet, can drastically affect crop production. Some years may be very good and enable a surplus of crops to be produced. On the other hand, some years may bring drought or insect infestations, and not enough food is produced, causing shortages.

Food surpluses and shortages are always important factors in determining whether people throughout the world have enough to eat. One of the major functions of governments is to make sure there is enough food for everyone. Governments encourage farmers to produce slightly more food than is needed in a normal season to allow for the years when there is a poor harvest.

The concept of surplus and shortage is a balancing act, however. If farmers produce too much food, they lose money because they cannot sell it all. If this happens, farmers are likely to produce less food the following year, so they will not lose more money. If that year sees a bad harvest, however, there will likely be a food shortage and prices will rise dramatically; some people will go hungry and starve. Because of this delicate balance, governments have become involved in the raising and marketing of agriculture. If they did not, the unpredictable cycle of surplus and shortage could cause national, and even worldwide, disasters.

Some governments set target prices for basic staple foods. To protect farmers, imports are not allowed to come into the country at lower prices. If they did, it would hurt the local farmers and markets. If there is a surplus in a particular year and prices fall, the government can intervene by buying surplus food and taking it off the market for storage to be used later during years of shortage.

By controlling food availability through **quotas** as well as prices, governments can protect farmers—especially those that work small farms or have to transport their goods great distances—and ensure that enough food will be produced to feed everyone. As a result, farmers will have successful businesses and continue to produce more food.

The less-developed countries have a completely different problem. In their societies, there is not enough food available to go around. Famine and starvation unfortunately occur often. Many people in these countries are continually malnourished, which causes a variety of other health-related problems. Wars and natural disasters—such as the devastating tsunami that struck Asia in December 2004—also cause situations where victims need emergency aid, in the form of supplies and food.

Over the years, huge amounts of money and aid have been designated to help starving people in Africa, Eastern Europe, and other countries. Food aid is often sent to help these people, but it is not without its own problems. Sometimes the countries that need help the most are located far away from major shipping ports. Sometimes food must travel hundreds of miles to reach the people who need it the most. It is often difficult to get the food to these people. Several scientists and government planners have suggested that permanent food storage areas be built in these countries.

While supplying food and other goods to needy nations is necessary and helpful, many believe that sending aid is only a short-term fix rather than a permanent solution. The long-term solution lies in educating farmers in underdeveloped countries and providing economic assistance so that they can increase the productivity of their own land through the use of machinery, fertilizers, and conservation farming practices.

GLOBAL AGRIBUSINESS

To become competitive in today's global marketplace, farmers need to be a part of the chain of production—from the farm to the grocery store. Factors such as inefficient transportation and lack of economic information can make it difficult for farmers to become competitive in the global marketplace.

Today, instead of being separated by distance, transportation, and communication barriers, nations have become interdependent (dependent on each other for specific resources). These resources include commodities, such as coffee, tea, citrus fruits, vegetables, chocolate, spices, and many others.

The United States is the world's leading agricultural exporter and the third-largest food importer in the world. World trade began to expand in the 1960s, when America realized the plight of starving people throughout the world. Around the same time, the American economy needed new export earnings to counteract the rising costs of imported oil. In the 1970s, U.S. farmers geared up to meet world demands.

Trade among nations is one of the ways to expand food supplies and reduce food costs. Trade is also important because many of the most heavily populated areas of the world are not agricultural areas. Weather also plays a role—if one area experiences a drought and a poor harvest, the people in that area must trade with another country whose crop was successful.

Out of approximately 190 countries worldwide, less than a dozen produce enough food for their own populations; these are primarily

The People Behind Pizza

Think for a minute about your favorite foods and the processes that had to take place to get them to you. For example, next time you eat a slice of pizza, ask yourself how many people helped bring that pizza to you. Consider the following:

Pizza crust The flour in the crust required a growing season for the wheat as well as harvesting, processing, inspecting, storing, and shipping it to the distributor that the pizza maker bought it from.

Pizza sauce The tomatoes in the sauce required a growing season, harvesting, inspecting, and shipping to a distributor. The spices in the sauce (such as oregano, basil, garlic, and caraway seed) required a growing season, harvesting, inspecting, processing, and shipping to a distributor.

Cheese This required a cow being milked; the milk being pasteurized, homogenized, and processed into cheese; inspection; packaging; and shipping to a distributor.

Meat toppings This required the raising of livestock for pork, beef, chicken, or fish over the span of their lives (including growing of their food); shipping to the meat packing plant to be processed; inspection; packaging; and shipping to a distributor.

Vegetable and fruit toppings Toppings, such as peppers, onions, and mushrooms, required a growing season, harvesting, inspecting, processing, transporting, and shipment to a distributor. Olives or pineapple required a growing season, harvesting, inspecting, processing, and transporting to a distributor. The pineapple may have been grown in a distant location, such as Hawaii or Korea, and transported a great distance to the United States.

The making of your pizza directly, or indirectly, involved many, many people. Now, think about tacos, a banana split, macaroni and cheese, a hamburger, or french fries. Figure it out, and you may never look at food in the same way again.

the major developed countries of the world. About 50 nations are nearly self-sufficient, but almost 130 are dependent on outside food sources. The biggest U.S. export products include agricultural, fishery, and forestry products. According to the U.S. Department of Agriculture, the largest U.S. imports (what the United States buys from other countries) include coffee, meat, lumber, tropical oils, spices, fruits, and vegetables.

When farmers become involved in a global market by exporting goods, they must be willing to commit a lot of time and energy to the endeavor. In order to be an exporter, a farmer must be able to do several jobs. He or she must be an analyst, a sales representative, and an expert in cultural differences. Before becoming involved in global trade, farmers must conduct market research in order to decide where to sell their goods. Some of the issues that farmers must consider include the following:

- Economics of the prospective country
- The country's purchasing potential
- Product demand and suitability
- The country's legal system
- The country's culture
- Language barriers
- Political stability

There are many ways for farmers to enter the global market. To assist farmers, there are organizations that can help, such as export management companies (EMCs) and export trading companies (ETCs). Export companies generally have better connections and expertise in overseas dealings.

Some farmers form cooperatives. A cooperative is an organization where the members work together toward a common goal. Cooperatives can provide market research, producer education, and greater purchasing power. Another type of cooperative is the Foreign Agricultural Service. It is a program sponsored by the USDA, and helps

A loaded ship at dock is getting ready to transport goods internationally. Cargo containers stacked on top of each other are loaded and unloaded with a crane. *(Courtesy of the U.S. Department of Agriculture)*

farmers that wish to export products and participate in international commerce.

Many commodities must be shipped under refrigeration to counter ripening; softening; dehydration; spoilage; and texture, flavor, or color changes. Transportation methods are a critical component of trading agricultural commodities globally. Selection of the most cost-effective route for the transport of freight from its point of origin to its destination is one of the most crucial decisions an exporter makes. The transportation of U.S. agricultural products to their overseas markets generally requires the selection and use of the fastest and most efficient mode of transportation.

Transportation is the critical link between the farmer and the consumer. Technological developments have changed the service capabilities and cost factors associated with the transportation of goods. The development of the intermodal van container was one of the most important breakthroughs in transportation technology for overseas shipments of agricultural perishables. The container is a storage compartment that is 40 feet (12.2 meters) long. It is highly adaptable—it can be moved by railroad, truck, ship, or airplane. It is beneficial because it protects the merchandise as it is shipped. This type of container also reduces labor costs, because compared to other types of shipping containers, it is easy to handle at shipping ports and train yards.

FOOD PROGRAMS—NATIONAL AND INTERNATIONAL

It is estimated that about 800 million people in the world lack an adequate, dependable food supply. A United States government program called USAID: Food for Peace, has instituted five-year development projects to increase agricultural productivity as well as emergency food assistance programs to help those in need. Assistance projects, in addition to including immediate food items, include programs to improve soil fertility, create adequate water supplies (with wells and reservoirs), and increase the fertility of the ground through the conservation methods that will be discussed in Chapter 8. USAID's goal is to establish food security, which they define as "when all people at all times have both physical and economic access to sufficient food to meet their dietary needs for a productive and healthy life." USAID provides government-to-government grants to support long-term agricultural growth.

USAID also assists with the construction of roads, transport, and storage facilities for countries in need, as well as offering education programs in agribusiness practices so that developing countries can provide for themselves. The organization works with all participants in agricultural development to support efforts to increase productivity— from farmers to scientists working to develop new, more productive varieties of seeds. USAID works with agribusinesses that want to develop new markets as well as governments, and it provides a legal framework in which to do business. The organization also works with universities and researchers to develop new technologies, as well as with local communities to teach them how to manage their available natural resources for sustainable agricultural production.

There are also domestic food programs in place to help the needy obtain the food they need for themselves and their families, such as the Food Stamp Program. The National School Lunch Program, available in schools is another example of a successful food program. President Harry S. Truman signed the National School Lunch Act on June 4, 1946. This act authorized the National School Lunch Program. The act was initially passed in response to claims that many American men had been rejected for World War II military service because of diet-related health problems. The federally assisted meal program was put in place as "a measure of national security, to safeguard the health and well-being of the nation's children and to encourage the domestic consumption of nutritious agricultural commodities."

Today, public schools, private schools, and child-care centers can participate in the National School Lunch Program. The program also offers snacks as well as a breakfast program. The School Breakfast Program was established by President Lyndon B. Johnson in 1966, when he signed the Child Nutrition Act.

BRINGING FARMING HOME

A U.S. organization called the 4-H Club gives young people practical experience with rural lifestyles as well as an opportunity to experience personal growth. The 4-H Club began around the start of the twentieth century as a result of the work of several people in different parts of the United States who were concerned about young people's futures. The practical, hands-on learning environment was established in order to make public school education more connected to country life. It was initially designed to help rural youths.

A 4-H Club horseshow at the Anne Arundel County Fair. (*Courtesy of the U.S. Department of Agriculture; photo by Bill Tarpenning*)

At the same time, college instructors, researchers, and the USDA realized that many farming adults did not accept new agricultural discoveries. They were reluctant to change the farming practices they were used to. These educators found that youths would experiment with new ideas and then share their experiences and successes with adults.

This marked the beginning of rural youth programs whose influence introduced new agricultural technology to adults. A youth group started in Ohio in 1902 by A.B. Graham is considered the birth of the 4-H program. In 1914, Congress created the Cooperative Extension Service at the USDA, which included both boys' and girls' club work. This began the 4-H Club.

Over the years, 4-H has evolved into a broader, more inclusive program. In the 1950s, 4-H began to extend into urban areas. The organization had also established an international connection with youths of other countries through the International Farm Youth Exchange Program. Later, the focus of 4-H Clubs became the

4-H: What Does It Symbolize?

The four Hs stand for the following:

- Head—Thinking critically; solving problems.
- Heart—Respecting self, others, and the environment; communicating.
- Hands—Preparing for a career; serving others.
- Health—Choosing healthy lifestyles; managing change and challenges.

The 4-H motto: To make the best better.

The 4-H pledge: I pledge my head to clearer thinking, my heart to greater loyalty, my hands to larger service, and my health to better living, for my club, my community, my country, and my world.

personal growth of the member. Life skills development was built into 4-H projects, activities, and events to help youths become contributing, productive, self-directed members of society. Today, members can participate and compete in many different programs ranging from farm activities, sewing, leadership, horsemanship, training pets, repairing computers, and growing plants to building rockets. Anyone can become a member and participate, regardless of where they live.

MANAGEMENT OF THE LAND, WATER, SOIL, AND ENVIRONMENT

Agriculture involves many natural elements: rivers, lakes, fields, plants, soil, animals, chemical systems, ecosystems, and wildlife habitats, to name a few. Each has its own specific requirements in order to stay healthy. Sometimes, overuse of one of these elements or mismanagement of one or more can cause negative impacts on the other elements. Like a giant jigsaw puzzle, if one piece is damaged or destroyed, it affects the entire picture.

Farmers must continually look for ways to manage these natural resources in order to maintain a productive agricultural system. They must not only be concerned with the health of their land, but must also look at the bigger picture in order to expect a productive future. Because impact in one area can cause a domino effect in other areas, management is indeed a delicate balancing act. This chapter examines natural resources and agricultural management, pertinent management issues, the Agricultural Environment Management System, and **agroforestry**.

NATURAL RESOURCES AND AGRICULTURAL MANAGEMENT

Agricultural management today focuses mainly on an integrated natural resources approach. In other words, the best management practices are those that take all natural resources into account. Farmers must look beyond their farms and view management decisions on a broader landscape level. For example, decisions about irrigation and other water use should be assessed by looking at the entire **watershed** area of the landscape—the concept that there is always someone downstream and that poor management decisions will impact everyone else that receives the water afterward.

Responsible management for the twenty-first century includes employing practices that use the land to meet present needs and protect its long-term quality. Because of this, technologies and farming practices are continually being developed in the search for ways to mesh diverse land uses, such as crop production, livestock production, forestry, wildlife protection, water quality maintenance, and soil quality.

Researchers and farmers are working more closely together to achieve this. The key to successful management is landowners, universities, and government/public agencies working together to achieve a common goal. This is especially important as the amount of farmland and grazing land is reduced, as urbanization continues to spread. It is critical to manage the land wisely in order to conserve the available resources. For example, soil must be managed, high water quality must be maintained, salinity must be monitored and controlled, manure must be managed appropriately, and the health of plants and animals must be monitored and regulated.

A healthy environmental approach includes maintaining irrigation ditches and reservoirs to keep them from becoming polluted, cutting water use and significantly reducing soil erosion (up to 95% by using center-pivot irrigation systems), fencing cropland and riparian areas to reduce damage from grazing livestock, converting less-productive cropland back to grassland, and eliminating noxious weeds.

MANAGEMENT ISSUES

This section will explore several management issues, such as soil management, water quality management, chemical management, salinity management, manure management, and animal/plant health management.

Soil Management

Although there are many different types of soils, there are common factors that determine whether or not the soil is healthy. Healthy soil must have the following properties:

- It must be able to promote biological activity, diversity, and productivity.
- It must regulate water flow.

Who Manages What?

In the United States, various federal agencies have been established to oversee different agricultural products and practices and to ensure high standards of quality. The following agencies are actively promoting safe and productive agriculture in the following ways:

Agency	Products/Practices Regulated	Safety Standards
United States Food and Drug Administration (FDA)	Food, food additives, animal feed, veterinary drugs	Making sure foods are safe to eat
United States Department of Agriculture (USDA)	Plants, plant pests	Making sure plants are safe to grow
United States Environmental Protection Agency (EPA)	Microbial/plant pesticides, new uses of existing pesticides, microorganism research	Safety of the environment, safety of herbicides and pesticides

- It must filter, buffer, and detoxify both organic and inorganic materials.
- It must store and cycle nutrients and other elements within the Earth's biosphere.

The concept of soil quality refers to the chemical, biological, and physical characteristics of the soil that allow it to perform these four critical functions. Soil is a working system.

The microorganisms (bacteria and fungi) in soils, and other animals (such as earthworms) play an important role in getting nutrients to crops. They help deliver nutrients by decomposing soil organic matter and releasing plant nutrients. They also improve the structure of the soil by mixing and churning the particles, which serves to increase water flow to plants as well as to keep the soil's structure loose enough that plant roots can penetrate the ground easier.

The level of carbon dioxide in the soil is also critical for healthy soil. This is called the soil respiration rate. The more available oxygen there is in the soil, the better. Oxygen becomes limited when soils are saturated with water. Soils with a looser structure encourage more oxygen circulation. In order to achieve this, farmers often mix organic materials into the soil. They must also be careful not to overwater their fields if they want their soil to remain healthy.

Other soil properties can be managed to create healthy soils. The bulk density, water holding capacity, and porosity (open spaces in the soil) can all be improved. Bulk density is the combination of air space, minerals (inorganic materials), and organic materials. By controlling the soil's bulk density, farmers can reduce soil erosion and leaching of nutrients and increase crop productivity. Bulk density determines the way the soil can store water as well as how much water it can store at a given time. If soil has a proper bulk density, runoff and erosion losses of soil and nutrients can be controlled.

Farmers can periodically test their soil to determine its fertility. According to the USDA Natural Resources Conservation Service, the following are the most important soil factors:

- Soil pH: An acceptable range is between 5.5 and 7.8 on the pH scale (soils should not be too acidic).
- Fertility level: Fertilizers can be added to increase fertility.
- Organic matter: The soil should have 3% to 8% organic matter.
- Salinity: The amount of salt in the soil and water should be low, or it will kill the crops (most crops cannot tolerate salt).
- Bulk density: Farmers need soils with a good mix of air space, minerals, and organic matter.
- Water-holding capacity: Crops do better in soils that can hold more water.

These are the things farmers look at when they manage their farms. These factors are also areas that can be adjusted to make the soil more fertile.

When soil needs more organic matter, mulches or soil amendments can be added. A soil amendment is something that is mixed into the soil, using a tiller or spade, to improve the soil's texture or structure. Mulch is applied in a thick layer on top of the soil. Organic mulches help plant growth in many ways. Because natural mulches come from existing plant material, they decompose naturally into the soil. Mulches keep the soil from clumping together. Mulch also protects the soil against erosion from rain or irrigation. Mulches keep the temperature of the soil under control. They act like an insulating blanket, keeping much of the sun's heat from drying out the soil. They also keep excessive water from evaporating, making sure the upper layers of soil have enough moisture. They protect crops by giving the roots access to the richest layers of the soil while controlling weeds. Common materials used as mulches and amendments include fir bark, chipped wood, dry lawn clippings, manure, and mushroom compost.

Researchers even use remote sensing (a science that uses images taken from satellites or photos taken from airplanes) in soil management. Images can be used to estimate the presence and concentration of salts in soil in specific areas of a pasture. This data can be entered into a Geographic Information System (GIS) along with other spatial data (such as crop type, locations of streams and wells, and slope of the land) to build a scientific computer model to locate, monitor, and manage subareas of a pasture and predict and correct localized problems. This may be done in a precision agriculture application.

Computer models can also be developed to evaluate, predict, and manage the movement of water, agricultural chemicals, and the movement of pesticides from agricultural fields to surface water and groundwater. By establishing working models, scientists give farmers tools to help them manage their land, improve production, and conserve resources.

Researchers are also working with plant genetics to develop a better understanding of salt tolerance in crop plants that will lead to the development of crops that are more salt tolerant and easier to grow in salt-affected soils.

Water Quality Management

Sometimes water contamination is due to natural causes, but other times it is due to human-induced causes such as agriculture. Scientists, farmers, and land managers must look at water quality on the scale of the entire watershed, not just specific areas within the watershed. The entire system must be managed as a unit; everything is connected and pollution at one source can cause problems at another point in the watershed.

Agriculture is the single-largest use of freshwater resources. Except for water lost through evapotranspiration, agricultural water is recycled back to surface water and groundwater. Agriculture, however, can be a cause and a victim of water pollution. It can cause pollution by contaminating water with chemicals (from pesticides and fertilizers), sediments (from eroded soil), adding salts to water, water logging irrigated land, introducing animal waste, introducing fuel oil and hazardous products used in farming, or introducing by-products used in agricultural processing. Agriculture can be a victim of pollution if irrigation water is already polluted and contaminates the crops being irrigated.

Water quality is a global issue—it affects agriculture everywhere. Maintaining high water quality is an important management issue for farmers because it involves environmental, economic, and health concerns. There are two types of water pollution: point-source pollution and non-point-source pollution. Point-source pollution is pollution that originates from a specific location or is a result of a specific activity. This type of pollution is much easier to correct and manage. Non-point-source pollution is pollution that comes from many areas or sources at once. There is no obvious point of entry into the system. This type of pollution is much harder to identify and control.

Examples of agricultural sources of non-point-source pollution include animal feedlots, irrigation systems, cultivation techniques, pastures, dairy farming, orchards, and aquaculture. Runoff water from many of these uses can contaminate surface water and groundwater. Irrigation can return salts, nutrients, and pesticides to groundwater. Non-point-source pollutants are transported over land and through the soil by rainwater and melting snow. These pollutants eventually find their way into groundwater, wetlands, rivers, lakes, and, finally, to oceans in the form of sediment and chemical loads carried by rivers. The EPA has identified agriculture as the leading cause of non-point-source water pollution in the United States. It is also the leading cause of groundwater pollution. The leading causes of agricultural impact on water quality are detailed in the table on page 126.

These types of pollution can adversely affect habitats and human health. Problems also occur when nutrients from fertilizers and animal wastes are applied to farmland in quantities that exceed the amount actually used by the crop or the amount that can be held by the soil. Farmers must manage their farms to lessen these impacts. They must manage pests, nutrients and waste, vegetative and tillage practices, and structural practices. If pesticides are applied only in the specific areas they are needed and in amounts that can be used completely, farmers can manage pests better and decrease pollution.

Effective nutrient management, such as applying nutrients only when needed and in the quantities that plants can use, is another way to manage the water. Good management practices for vegetative and tillage practices include contour farming, using correct cropping sequences, and using natural windbreaks. These will be discussed in

Agricultural Impact on Water Quality

Agricultural Activity	Impact
Tilling	Adds sediments and chemicals to water sources.
Manure spreading	Introduces pathogens (such as E. coli), phosphorus, and nitrogen into the water.
Fertilizing	Runoff nutrients can get into the public water supply and make the water taste bad. Algae growth can kill fish.
Pesticides	Can affect the health of fish and other wildlife and cause reproductive failure and poor growth.
Feedlots/Corrals	Introduce pathogens—bacteria and viruses— and metals into the water supply. Can increase levels of ammonia.
Irrigation	Can add salts to the water supply as well as trace elements that may be harmful to human health.
Clear cutting	Removing native vegetation can lead to soil erosion and sediment pollution in the water.

Source: Food and Agriculture Organization of the United Nations

more detail later in this chapter and in Chapter 8. Good structural management processes include terracing, grading (slope stabilization), and sediment control basins. These are considered conservation measures and will also be discussed in the next chapter. Wells can be treated with chlorine to enhance the quality of water, especially for human consumption. These types of farming measures are often referred to as best management practices, or BMPs.

Agricultural producers are realizing that improved water quality can increase productivity and reduce the costs of maintaining water systems. There are many benefits of clean water for farming. For example, clean water helps the livestock industry. It has been shown that cattle that drink poor-quality water do not gain as much weight and are more susceptible to poor health than cattle that drink unpolluted water. In order to keep cattle from polluting water sources, some farmers use solar-powered water pumping systems to fill drinking troughs that are placed away from water sources, rather than letting the cattle drink directly from streams.

Chemical Management

Managing the use of pesticides, herbicides, and fertilizers is critical in responsible farm management. Following World War II, farmers relied heavily on long-acting, nonselective (affects many life forms, not just the specific ones of interest) pesticides. Over the years, farmers and scientists realized that this approach was not the best solution for the environment as a whole. As a result, better, more selective pesticides have been developed. Pesticides have also become shorter acting (so that chemical effects do not linger in the soil and in other areas of the environment) and safer. These have been beneficial changes in the use of chemicals.

In addition to monitoring and controlling pesticides, it is also important to look at the degradates of pesticides. Degradates are the products that the parent pesticide transforms into once it enters the environment. They are generally various forms of acid. They can present a problem if they get into the water supply. Monitoring and managing the presence and effect of the degradates is as important as monitoring the actual pesticide.

Farmers can follow an established process that leads toward effective management of chemicals. They begin the process by having their soil tested to find out what they need to do in order to grow the crop they want, and then they select the specific fertilizers that will give them the best results. When applying fertilizers, several management techniques can be used, such as applying multiple small doses rather than one or two large ones, testing existing nutrient levels in the soil before adding more, or concentrating fertilizer near crop roots instead of spreading it evenly all over the ground.

When herbicides are used to control weeds, many farmers try to use as many biological controls as possible, such as crop rotation, planting cover crops, and spacing rows of crops closer together. Using post-emergent herbicides is also a common management decision. This involves using an herbicide once the weeds are already growing. By doing so, the farmer can see which specific areas need the herbicide and treat only those areas. Another management alternative for controlling weeds is called clean farming. This involves using hedgerows and grasses to control weed infestation. It can also include taking advantage of native habitat that harbors the insects and wildlife that prey on pests in areas close to fields.

Some farmers manage application of fertilizers by collecting soil samples, having them analyzed, and plotting their locations on a map through the use of GPS technology. Once the exact locations are plotted on a map, they can be used in a computer to model crop nutrient needs. Nutrient recommendation maps can then be used to develop fertilizer recommendation maps, which can then be uploaded to a fertilizer applicator's GPS-enabled controller. The end result is a near-perfect application of fertilizer. Comparing yields from one year to the next for specific areas can lead to a realistic production plan for different areas within a field. This is another example of precision farming.

Salinity Management

Salinity is a measure of the total amount of salt in the water. When salt levels are too high, this can cause a salinity hazard. Too much salt in the soil or water can reduce water availability to a crop. Because of this, crop yields can be significantly reduced.

Controlling salinity in water sources for livestock is also important. Animals do not do well drinking water with significant salt content levels. Salt can cause health problems and keep livestock from gaining weight. In order to control salinity, soil and water need to be closely monitored.

Manure Management

In livestock operations, whether they deal with cattle, sheep, goats, chickens, turkeys, or any other type of animal, manure accumulation can become a problem. One of the largest concerns is manure contaminating the water supply. This can happen after heavy rainfall on freshly fertilized fields or if manure collects near a water source. Contamination can be controlled if manure is kept in a secure (non-leaking) container or by keeping livestock away from water sources.

One way to deal with manure is to turn it into an asset. Some farmers divide their pastures into smaller grazing areas. Moving livestock from one area to another lets the manure be dispersed evenly instead of collecting in one area. The manure is then used as fertilizer. Other farmers keep their livestock confined in a barn and collect the manure over time. They can use this supply as natural fertilizer when they need it.

Animal and Plant Health

The Animal and Plant Health Inspection Service in the USDA is responsible for protecting America's animal and plant resources from agricultural pests and diseases. Inspections are crucial. If they were not conducted, the possible threats to our food supply and to the economy would be huge. If APHIS did not check for, and prevent, agricultural pests such as the Mediterranean fruit fly, from entering the country, those pests would cause billions of dollars in production loss in this country. If pests were not checked for and eliminated, they could infect huge amounts of food. APHIS also inspects for the presence of livestock diseases. A recent example of this is the detection of mad cow disease (called bovine spongiform encephalopathy). If this disease were allowed to spread, it could devastate the livestock industry.

All food in the United States goes through strict regulation and inspection processes to ensure its safety. Restaurants and food chains also impose strict regulations on the food they prepare and sell to ensure consistent high quality. These inspections and the role of APHIS are critical not only for the economy of the United States, but also for global trade.

Nature's Micromanagers

Worms are one of the soil's best friends. Earthworms are critical for the health of gardens and farmland. Because they are constantly tunneling through soil, they help bring in oxygen, drain water, and create space for plant roots. Worm manure (called casts) is also rich in nutrients.

Some worms—such as Aporrectodea and Lumbricus—can also adapt to different types of soils and temperatures. If it gets too cold, they tunnel deeper into the soil before it gets too hard. They can also go into a sleeplike state called estivation—similar to hibernation. When they go into estivation, they coil into a slime-coated ball. They can survive in frozen and dry soils through estivation. When conditions improve, they become active again in the soil.

Scientists believe that earthworms were originally introduced to America from Europe. They believe worms were brought over in seed stock and potted plants. A modern-day descendent of the worms from Europe are the night crawlers. Today, they are found all over America and are some of the largest worms around—they can grow to be 8 inches (20 centimeters) or more. They are also very fast because they spend a lot of the time at the surface of the soil and have learned to be quick to avoid birds and other predators.

Each type of worm has different strengths and weaknesses, and therefore plays a different role in agriculture. But all worms are important for mixing soil, adding nutrients, and providing a healthy environment for plants.

AGRICULTURAL ENVIRONMENTAL MANAGEMENT SYSTEMS

Similar to managing anything else, in order to manage a farm, the farmer must have a good management plan, preferably one that not only takes production into account, but is also environmentally wise and provides for sustainable agriculture. This type of plan is called an agricultural environmental management system (AEMS).

A management plan includes methods to manage pests, nutrients, and manure. It deals with monitoring and testing the soil, chemical applications (such as pesticides), and livestock feeding requirements. It addresses all the issues that go into running a farm, both in the short term and long term. It addresses environmental concerns—such as water quality, erosion, and soil fertility—as well as improving the overall management of the farm.

The best management plans are those that are always evolving. Plans identify and prioritize environmental concerns, identify steps that need to be taken, and set measurable directives so that the farmer can tell whether or not the plan is working. This approach allows the farmer to determine how the farm affects the environment, how to tell if the plan is working, and then develop action plans for the things that still need work. The farmer can look at impacts on soil, air, water, and other natural resources. The farmer can also implement emergency plans and determine which types of farming practices might work best on his or her farm (such as crop rotation, terracing, or agroforestry).

Once a farmer develops and implements a plan, the plan must constantly be reviewed and assessed. If there is room to improve, improvements are made. The plan continues to be assessed, and as advancements in technology occur, changes to the plan can be made.

All plans are unique, because they deal with a specific farm, but all good plans share common elements. They are all devised to prevent pollution, follow environmental regulations, and continually strive to improve. Many farmers claim that having a working management plan has allowed them to become more aware of environmental issues and has also reduced the amount of work they do because it has made them more efficient. Because the plan improves the management of the farm, it also helps reduce the amount of money spent on fertilizers, pesticides, feed, or energy.

AGROFORESTRY

Agroforestry is a recent agricultural practice that is beginning to gain popularity. It is an intensive land management system that optimizes the benefits from the biological interactions that are created when trees or shrubs are deliberately combined with crops or livestock. It allows production of crops, trees, and livestock from the same piece of land.

Agroforestry also helps with resource conservation. For example, agroforestry helps control soil erosion and creates wildlife habitat. Agroforestry practices need to be tailored to easily fit in with farming practices—they should not impact existing crops, but instead should enhance the land's productivity. There are five basic types of agroforestry practices today in the United States: alley cropping, forest farming, riparian buffers, silvopasture, and windbreaks.

Alley Cropping

Alley cropping combines trees planted in single or grouped rows, with agricultural or horticultural crops that are cultivated in the wide alleys between the tree rows. Commonly used trees are the high-value hardwoods (such as walnut, ash, or oak), fruit trees, nut trees, or fast-growing species (such as hybrid poplar). The most common crops grown in the alleyways between the trees are row crops (corn, soybean, or specialty crops, such as herbal or medicinal plants), forages, and vegetables. The cultivated crops provide the farmer with extra income while waiting for the trees to bear fruit or mature.

There are several benefits of alley cropping. It is one way for farmers to convert marginal cropland into woodland and still make a profit from the crops. In areas where erosion is a problem, introducing trees increases the value of the land. The rows of trees also function as windbreaks. This not only helps prevent damage in the crop alleys by controlling wind erosion, but the trees also create a sheltered microclimate that improves the yield and quality of the crops. Alley cropping also increases the biodiversity of cropland, which creates new habitat for wildlife.

Forest Farming

Forest farming is the intentional cultivation of specialty crops beneath forest trees. The crops grown in the understory must be shade-loving plants that are naturally adapted to grow in forested conditions. The forest cover is usually modified to produce the correct level of shade for the crops.

Specialty crops can be those used for medicinal, ornamental, or culinary uses. Such crops include ginseng, decorative ferns, and

Living Snow Fences—Agriculture Working for You

Living snow fences are designed plantings of trees or shrubs and native grasses located along roads or ditches, or around communities and farmsteads. These plantings create a vegetative barrier that traps and controls blowing and drifting snow.

Living snow fences are especially helpful along roads because they can trap blowing snow and prevent snowdrifts on the road. They also help improve visibility by keeping snow from blowing across the road as well as reducing the buildup of slush and ice on the pavement. It is estimated that a living snow fence that is 10 feet (3 meters) tall can trap 20 to 30 tons of snow per linear foot.

In addition to trapping snow, living snow fences (like windbreaks) also provide better-functioning drainage systems and reduced spring flooding; improved wildlife habitat (birds and other wildlife); livestock protection; reduced soil erosion; and a reduction in energy costs to heat and cool homes.

mushrooms. Forest farming can provide a profitable side business for woodland forest owners, nut growers, and herb growers.

There are many benefits to forest farming. The cultivation of specialty crops in a forest setting provides an additional source of

Types of Agroforestry

(a) Alley cropping
Row crops are planted between widely-spaced rows of trees.

(b) Forest farming
The intentional cultivation of edible, medicinal, or specialty crops beneath native or planted forests.

(c) Riparian buffers
A strip of trees, bushes, or grasses planted between cropland/pasture and water sources.

(d) Silvopasture
The combination of trees, forage plants, and livestock together as an integrated system.

(e) Windbreaks
Linear plantings of trees or shrubs to control wind erosion.

© Infobase Publishing

Different types of agroforestry practices are shown here. (a) alley cropping; (b) forest farming; (c) riparian buffers; (d) silvopasture; (e) windbreaks.

income for the farmer. Crops can be repeatedly raised and sold during the years the trees must grow before they are big enough to harvest for timber. Forest farming is also ecologically responsible. If specialty forest plants (such as mushrooms) are grown intentionally to harvest, it is better for the environment than picking mushrooms in the wild, where they could become endangered.

Riparian Buffers

Riparian buffers are strips of trees, shrubs, and grass that are planted between cropland or pastures and surface watercourses (such as streams, lakes, wetlands, ponds, or drainage ditches).

Riparian buffers protect water quality. They are very effective at trapping and filtering sediments, nutrients, and chemicals in runoff from cropland and pastures. The plants in the buffer absorb nutrients and chemicals that would otherwise flow into adjacent streams, lakes, ponds, and other water sources. Buffers must be wide enough to slow down overland flow and allow time for nutrient uptake and sediment trapping to take place. They also degrade pesticides and control pollution by absorbing and filtering animal wastes.

Buffers also reduce soil erosion. The plants in riparian buffers help control soil erosion because they stabilize the soil with their roots. They also serve as a physical barrier to reduce overland water flow. They prevent cropland from flooding. Deep-rooted trees and shrubs stabilize stream banks, also reducing erosion and sediment transport. When grass is present, their roots spread out and bind the soil, reducing erosion. The grasses, because they are at ground level, also trap sediment.

Riparian buffers create habitats for aquatic and terrestrial wildlife. When large trees are next to streams, they moderate the stream temperature by providing shade. They also provide sources of large woody debris. Fish such as salmon need cool water temperatures and streambed gravel free of excess sediment in order to reproduce. Large fallen logs in the stream provide protection by creating places in which the fish can hide from predators.

An example of a riparian buffer in Madison County, Louisiana. The trees surround the lake and protect the water quality by filtering out contaminants from nearby fields. *(Courtesy of the U.S. Department of Agriculture; photo by Bill Tarpenning)*

The native shrubs and trees also provide birds and terrestrial animals with food, nesting sites, cover, and travel corridors. Riparian buffers can also provide a harvestable product, such as pulpwood, fruits, or nuts.

Silvopasture

Silvopasture is the intentional combination of trees, forage plants, and livestock as a single, intensively managed system. The wood from the trees can be harvested, and livestock can be produced, supported by grasses grown in the areas around the trees.

There are many benefits of silvopasture. The livestock provide the farmer with income while waiting for the trees to become big enough to harvest. Nitrogen-fixing forage species, pasture fertilization, and animal manure improve the soil and tree nutrition. Livestock grazing also helps control competing brushy species because the animals eat them. By eliminating an excess of brushy material, silvopasture also reduces the wildfire hazard. It is also better for the trees, because the more widely spaced from each other they are, the less the competition. This creates a better timber yield.

Trees create a sheltered microclimate that serves to protect animals from the heat and the cold. Shelter also improves the quality of the forage (what the livestock naturally eat) and lengthens the growing season, thereby increasing production. By actively pruning the trees, the farmer can, in turn, use the pruning as fodder (feed for livestock). This also results in better livestock growth.

Another benefit of silvopasture is that it creates a more biologically diverse system, which increases wildlife habitat. Cattle and sheep are the most common livestock used in silvopasture. Some nut and fruit orchards may also be grazed to produce income before the trees begin bearing.

Windbreaks

Windbreaks are linear plantings of trees and shrubs that are designed to enhance crop production, protect people and livestock, and benefit soil and water conservation. Windbreaks can be used by vine and fruit tree growers, row crop farmers, livestock producers, and rural homeowners around their homes and other buildings.

There are many benefits to using windbreaks. They provide microclimate modification. Field and orchard windbreaks can increase the yield of many different types of crops. They are especially valuable when farmers use them for high-value horticultural crops, such as raspberries, strawberries, and blueberries.

An example of conservation methods utilizing the silvopasture technique. The cattle graze the grass among the trees. They also keep the lower branches on the trees pruned, and their manure serves as fertilizer. *(Courtesy of the USDA Natural Resources Conservation Service; photo by Jeff Vanuga)*

Windbreaks can also be used as an integrated pest-management system. By introducing plants that attract beneficial insects, windbreaks can also serve to increase the biological control of crop insect pests. If trees and shrubs that produce specialty foods or decorative products are used in windbreaks—such as chokecherries or willow—they can provide extra income for the farmer.

Tree-sheltered areas can also play a large role in animal survival. Because windbreaks can modify harsh climatic conditions, they protect newborn animals from freezing. Windbreaks around feedlots have been shown to improve the health and weight gain of sheep and cattle in cold climates.

An example of conservation practices using field windbreaks in North Dakota. The vegetation windbreaks protect the soil against wind erosion. *(Courtesy of USDA Natural Resources Conservation Service; photo by Erwin Cole)*

If fast-growing species of trees are used in windbreaks, the farmer can produce and harvest timber for sale. Windbreaks are also helpful in reducing wind erosion. They protect fine-textured soils. In winter, they help disperse snow evenly across fields, making more moisture available for crops. They also help to control snow buildup when they are placed around buildings and alongside roadways.

Buildings, such as homes and offices, use 10% to 20% less energy for heating or cooling compared to unsheltered buildings, so windbreaks also assist in energy conservation. Windbreak trees and shrubs provide food and habitat for game birds and other wildlife. Windbreaks also assist in the carbon cycle. It is estimated that for each acre planted in field windbreaks more than 46,297 pounds (21 metric tons) of carbon dioxide will be stored in the trees by age 20.

CONSERVATION OF AGRICULTURAL RESOURCES

The Earth has a finite amount of arable land (able to grow crops). The success of agriculture depends on many factors—climate, temperature, moisture, soil type, topography (slope and landforms), economics, technology, development, population distribution, and natural resources, to name a few.

Agriculture can pose a delicate balancing act with natural ecosystems and biodiversity. Because farmers must produce food to survive, specific plants and animals for food and fiber must be cultivated and raised. In order to accomplish this on lands that are not only arable but also meet the right conditions for farming (such as those not impacted by population distribution and other land uses), ecosystems that have relatively high biodiversity must be replaced with agricultural ecosystems of relatively low biodiversity.

In order to maximize agricultural production and minimize economic expenditure, modern agriculture in the United States—and other developed countries—must rely heavily on the use of pesticides, fertilizers, and machinery in order to feed the world. Because this demand must be balanced by the need to protect the environment and maintain the health of the land, wise management techniques must be employed. If this does not happen, and the land's fertility is damaged, it may never recover. Soil-forming processes are so slow and nutrient cycling so delicate, environmental damage can have effects for many generations. Because of this, conservation of agricultural resources is a critical issue for farmers, land managers, and businesses, as well as everyone else on Earth.

RECYCLING, REDUCING, REUSING, AND SUSTAINABLE FARMING

Most farmers have long recognized the importance of protecting soil, water, and biological resources. Many farmers are conscientious stewards of the land. Still, as the world population continues to increase, stresses on natural resources will continue to increase as well. Only through active measures of conservation can natural resources be protected now and into the future.

In order for farmers to conserve resources, they must practice sustainable farming. They must use the land responsibly so that it can be productive in the present as well as the future. Because side effects of agriculture include loss of biodiversity and habitat, erosion and soil loss, soil contamination, possible degradation of water quality, and reduction of water quantity, conservative measures must be practiced. For example, recycling in agriculture can encompass managing the land so that as one crop depletes certain nutrients another can be planted afterward that replaces the lost nutrients. Crop rotation is an example of practical recycling.

Reducing impacts is also critical. By controlling erosion, controlling the amount of irrigation water used (by using water-efficient methods), or by controlling the amount of pesticides or fertilizers used, it is possible to reduce adverse environmental effects. Reusing resources is also environmentally responsible. Manure can be collected and reused as fertilizer instead of being left to seep into water sources and contaminate them. Composting is another method of reusing organic components to increase the fertility of agriculture.

Not only are recycling, reducing, and reusing important on the farm, they are also important downwind or downstream from the agricultural operation. Effects can often be far reaching—they can deplete aquifers or cause widespread impact on habitats. Conservation measures are important everywhere, but some areas are more at risk than others. The ability of a particular soil to erode depends on soil type, topography (slope of the land), organic matter, local geologic and erosive processes, and climate. Plowing destroys plant roots, which would otherwise help stabilize the soil. Soils that are disturbed by plowing and cultivation are prone to erosion by water runoff and wind.

In the United States, it is estimated that about 4 billion tons (about 3.6 trillion kilograms) of eroded sediment are deposited in waterways each year. Three-fourths of this is a result of agriculture. Scientists believe that currently one-third of the nation's topsoil has been lost to erosion. In some areas, soil erosion is as serious a problem as it was during the Dust Bowl of the 1930s. Sediments in waterways are a serious form of pollution, which can affect plants, animals, and human health by making water unfit for use.

Soil erosion can be reduced if farmland is allowed to recover by allowing it to remain fallow and letting natural succession take place, or by restoring native vegetation. Another viable solution is to remove highly erodible land from production. If land cannot be retired, there are many plowing and cultivation techniques that help conserve the land, such as contour plowing. Many of these techniques will be discussed in the next section. The success of various conservation techniques depends on local soil conditions, topography, and the type of crop that is being planted.

Another way that farmers can practice responsible conservation is to manage plant nutrients. As illustrated in the nutrient cycles, nutrients naturally cycle between water, air, soil, and biota. Agriculture can disrupt this natural cycling because it redistributes nutrients, depletes soils of some nutrients, and concentrates nutrients in eroded sediments and waterways.

In addition, many crops need great amounts of nutrients (like nitrogen and phosphorus), and they deplete the soil of them faster than the native plants in the area do. This necessitates the application of fertilizer, which must be carefully monitored. Harvesting crops also creates a nutrient sink. When the crop is completely removed, it cannot be recycled back into the system. Because of all these factors, farmers must pay close attention to the health of the soil. Soil surveys are conducted by the Natural Resources Conservation Service (NRCS) for the entire country. These surveys contain a wealth of information about local soil types and suggested land uses based on soil type in order to promote conservation and sustainable farming.

Another area of environmental concern is the effect of overgrazing on rangeland. In the United States, about 40% of the land is considered rangeland. If conservation measures are not practiced, overgrazing by livestock can alter plant communities by removing some species and allowing inedible species, invasive species, and noxious weeds, to take over. In many areas of the world, forests have been cleared and converted to rangeland/pasture, which has resulted in a significant loss of biodiversity and wildlife habitat. In some places it has changed the structure and function of the ecosystem.

Pest management is also an issue in proper conservation measures. When broad-spectrum pesticides are used (pesticides that affect a wide range of species, not a specific one) they can eliminate the beneficial species as well. For example, these pesticides can eliminate a pest's natural predator or plant pollinators. In addition, some pesticides are not readily biodegradable. Long after they have been used, the pesticides can collect in the tissues of plants and animals or in sediments. They can then reenter the food web and cause widespread problems. This is why many farmers who practice sustainable farming use some form of integrated pest management—a combination of several pest control techniques. If pesticides are used, the farmer carefully determines which specific pesticide will affect the pest, how much to use (so that it does not reside long-term in the environment), and when is the best time to apply it most effectively.

These types of conservation measures will enable long-term management of the land.

CONSERVATION MEASURES

Several agricultural conservation measures can be used to protect our natural resources. These include crop rotation; no-till, conservation tillage, and other crop residue management; the use of cover crops; terracing, grassed waterways, contour strip cropping, and contour buffer strips; erosion control and grade stabilization; and composting.

Crop Rotation

Crop rotation is the practice of changing the crops grown in a field, usually in a planned sequence. Crops need nutrients in order to grow. Grass plants—such as wheat, oats, and corn—use nitrogen to grow. Legumes—such as soybeans and alfalfa—have a **symbiotic** relationship with the nitrogen-fixing bacteria in the soil. The legumes and bacteria together create a form of nitrogen that is usable by the grass crops.

Because of this relationship, many farmers rotate their fields between grass and legume crops in order to keep a supply of nitrogen in the soil. Cover crops—such as clover and hay—are also cycled into the rotation in order to add organic material to the soil.

Crop rotation is also an effective way to control weeds, insects, and disease, because it naturally breaks the cycles of these different pests. It reduces soil erosion and saves fertilizer costs because the nitrogen that the grasses deplete is naturally added back into the soil by the legumes. It also reduces the potential for nitrate leaching to groundwater because the nitrogen is being actively produced and used from one planting to the next. This way, it does not build up.

No-till, Conservation Till, and Crop Residue Management

No-till agriculture is the practice of not plowing or disturbing the field. Because the soil is not disturbed, it minimizes the erosion and deposition of sediments into nearby water that plowing can cause. Instead, it ensures the soil is anchored to the plant root systems.

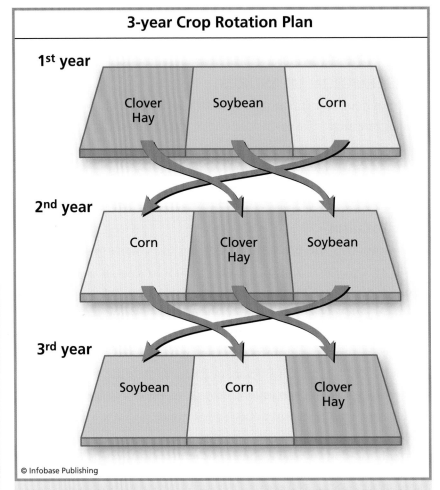

3-year Crop Rotation Plan

1st year

Clover Hay   Soybean   Corn

2nd year

Corn   Clover Hay   Soybean

3rd year

Soybean   Corn   Clover Hay

© Infobase Publishing

An example of crop rotation on a three-year rotation cycle using clover hay, soybean, and corn.

Conservation tillage is a management practice that minimizes soil disturbance. It provides long-term crop residues and vegetation on croplands. It reduces erosion and surface runoff of pesticides and heavy metals.

Both methods retain the crop residue and vegetative cover, which keeps the soil cooler longer and allows it to retain more moisture. They also enhance the fertility of the soil. Crop residue management is any tillage method that leaves crop residue on the surface to reduce the effects of erosion. The residue acts as a protective layer that shields the soil from wind and rain until the emerging crops are able to provide their own protective canopy. Crop residue improves soil **tilth** and adds organic matter to the soil. Less tillage also reduces soil compaction.

Cover Crops

A cover crop is a close-growing crop that temporarily protects the soil during the time before the next crop is established. Commonly used cover crops include oats, winter wheat, and cereal rye. Legume cover crops add nitrogen to the soil and provide low-cost fertilizer for future grain crops. They are planted as soon as possible after the harvest on fields where residue cannot sufficiently protect the soil from water and wind erosion during the winter and spring months.

A cover crop can also be planted after the last cultivation in order to provide a longer growing period. In sandy soils, they can be used to reduce nitrate leaching. Cover crops are very helpful with crops that do not provide a lot of residue, such as soybeans or corn. They are also beneficial on land that is easily erodible.

Terracing

A terrace is an earthen embankment that follows the contour of a hillside. It breaks a long slope into shorter segments like a set of stair steps. Terraces also intercept the flow of water by serving as small dams on a hillside. The terraces intercept runoff water and either help guide it to a safe outlet or are designed to collect the water and temporarily store it until it can filter into the ground. Some terraces are designed to serve as a channel in order to slow runoff and carry it to a designated outlet, such as a grassed waterway.

Terraces are effective on steep slopes because they reduce and control erosion. They can also serve as nesting habitats for birds. The cropland widths between terraces are usually just wide enough for the planting equipment to be able to move along them.

Grassed Waterways

A grassed waterway is a natural drainage way that is established with grass in order to prevent gullies from forming in fields. The natural drainage way is graded and shaped to form a smooth, shallow channel. It is then planted with grass so that a thick sod covers the drainage way.

The grass also serves a second purpose. It can trap sediment washed from the cropland, absorb any chemicals, heavy metals and nutrients contained in the runoff water and also provide cover for small birds and animals.

Each grassed waterway is slightly different—the design depends on the nature of the field it drains.

Contour Strip Cropping

Contour strip cropping is the practice of planting various row crops and hay (or small grains) in alternating strips planted side by side. Tilling and planting carry across the slopes, following the contour of the land.

When farming is done on the contour, it creates small ridges that slow runoff water (similar to the contouring practice discussed earlier). When the water is slowed, it has time to infiltrate the ground and it filters the sediments. Farming on the contour, rather than up or down the slope, also reduces wear and tear on the farm equipment and reduces fuel consumption.

Crop rotation also takes place with this farming method. Over successive years, the hay strips are rotated with the grain and crops. Rotating strips from corn to legumes allows the corn to use the nitrogen added to the soil by the legumes. It also reduces soil loss by 50% because the different crops alternating in different areas of the soil strengthen the soil characteristics over time. This way, the soil resources are not being depleted, as they would be if only one crop was ever grown on that area of land (there would be no nutrient exchange and natural balancing).

The ends of the rows are often planted with grasses in order to reduce erosion and make it easier to turn equipment. In areas where runoff is concentrated, grassed waterways can be used.

(Top) An aerial view of a field buffer and grass waterway system. *(Courtesy of the U.S. Department of Agriculture; photo by Tim McCabe)*
(Bottom) A field showing contour strip cropping. *(Courtesy of the U.S. Department of Agriculture)*

Contour Buffer Strips

Contour buffer strips are strips of grass or other permanent vegetation in a contoured field that trap sediment, pollutants, and nutrients (such as from fertilizers). Sediments can be kept from moving within farm fields and from farm fields. It is similar to contour strip cropping except that the permanent grass strips are narrower than the hay/grain strips used in contour strip cropping.

This conservation solution works well because the buffer strips are established along the contour of the land (they logically follow the direction of the slopes instead of running up or down the slopes sideways). Because of this, runoff flows slowly and evenly across the grass strips greatly reducing erosion. Vegetation is usually kept tall during spring runoff to slow it down and further control erosion. The vegetation is conservation oriented because it can provide wildlife habitat for small birds and other animals. Buffer strips are an inexpensive substitute for terraces.

Buffer strips can also be used in urban settings for the landscaping of yards on hills. There are also other advantages. They can improve soil, air, and water quality, restore biodiversity, and create scenic landscapes. They protect livestock from harsh weather and buildings from wind damage.

Many farmers have adopted conservation practices such as these because of initiatives led by the U.S. Natural Resources Conservation Service (NRCS), the Agricultural Research Service, the Farm Service Agency, the U.S. Forest Service, as well as other state and local conservation agencies. Several different types of buffer strips can be used for conservation purposes, including some of the previously discussed conservation measures. They include riparian buffers, grassed waterways, windbreaks, living snow fences, contour grass strips, shallow water areas for wildlife, shrub barriers, and alley cropping.

Erosion Control and Grade Stabilization

Grade-stabilization structures can be used in steep areas, such as gullies, to control and prevent erosion. A grade-stabilization structure can be an earthen or concrete structure built across a drainage way.

A dam, or embankment, built across the gully or grass waterway serves to drop the water to a lower elevation while protecting the soil from being scoured by running water. Dams are usually needed when the upstream area is unable to store excess water. Sometimes, farmers use the dams to store water. When they do this, it also provides a water source and habitat for wildlife. Dams must be well managed. Adequate soil conservation practices must be practiced upstream of the structure to avoid sedimentation.

Composting

Composting is a process of soil augmentation (creating a soil filler) that has been practiced throughout the ages. The Chinese people have collected and composted all the materials from their gardens, fields, and homes for thousands of years. Inhabitants of the Middle East over the ages have made compost as well.

Composting is a biological process in which microorganisms convert organic materials—such as leaves, paper, food, and manure—into a soil-like material called compost. Composting is a natural process that constantly occurs in nature. For example, in the fall, when leaves drop off the trees in forests, the leaves remain on the ground as forest litter and eventually become decomposed back into the ground. The particles mix with other organic material and work themselves into the soil, providing nutrients for the trees and other vegetation growing there.

Composting differs only slightly from this natural process. When humans purposely do it, the materials decompose faster.

Compost can be used for many things. It can be used as a source of manure handling and recycling. Manure is composted instead of being left on the ground to decompose. It keeps the manure from leaching nitrates and contaminating groundwater. It is also used to enhance soil and its fertility. It functions as a slow-acting fertilizer and not only supplies mineral elements to the soil—such as nitrogen, phosphorus, and calcium—but also helps improve soil structure as well as increase the soil's ability to hold and store water. When compost functions as a fertilizer, it eliminates the need to use chemical fertilizers. This is an environmentally friendly practice because it helps keep chemicals out of food sources.

Compost makes the soil healthier because it returns organic matter to the soil in a usable form. Organic matter in the soil improves plant

How to Build Your Own Compost System

Composting is a practical way to handle yard trimmings and the remains of garden plants. Kitchen scraps, such as fruit and vegetable peelings, eggshells, bread, and coffee grounds can also be used. Newspaper, cardboard, and sawdust are also beneficial. It is important, though, not to try to compost meat, bones, or fatty foods because they can attract rodents and other animals.

When preparing material for composting, the more surface area the microorganisms have to work on, the faster the material decomposes. Therefore, chopping up the material first into small pieces will speed the composting process.

A large compost pile insulates itself and holds the heat generated from the microbes working on decomposing the materials. Compost heaps that are 3 to 4 feet (0.9 to 1.2 meters) tall and wide work best. They need moisture and air to work properly.

Compost is usually contained within a bin that is set directly on the ground. Grass or other ground cover must be removed in the bin so that the compost pile can be in direct contact with the soil microorganisms. The bins can be made of several different materials: Woven wire fencing shaped into a circular enclosure is popular for backyard composting. A block bin can also be constructed. This is a three-sided box structure made by stacking cement blocks, bricks, or rocks. The building material is not cemented together, in order to allow the vital circulation of air within the compost heap. A square bin can also be constructed from wooden pallets wired together. Once the bin is prepared, compost can be added as follows:

growth by encouraging the growth of microorganisms that the plants can use and by loosening heavy clay soils so that plant roots can penetrate the ground easier. It also improves the capacity of the soil to hold water and nutrients, as well as add essential nutrients directly to the soil.

This method of fertilizing can be done by anyone, in a rural or urban area. When composting is done at home, yard trimmings such as grass clippings and kitchen scraps can be used. This helps the envi-

---

- First layer: 3 to 4 inches (7.6 to 10.2 centimeters) of chopped brush or other coarse material on top of the soil surface. This allows for proper air circulation.
- Second layer: 6 to 8 inches (15.2 to 20.3 cm) of mixed scraps, leaves, and grass clippings. Materials should be slightly damp.
- Third layer: 1 inch (2.5 centimeters) of soil. This adds microorganisms to the heap.
- Fourth layer: 2 to 3 inches (5 to 7.5 centimeters) of manure to provide nitrogen required by the microorganisms. Sprinkling wood ash or rock phosphate over the manure layer reduces the heap's acidity.

Keep repeating these layers until the bin is full, and then scoop out a "basin" at the top to catch rainwater. If the heap is made correctly, it will heat to 140° F (284° C) in five days. After three or four weeks, the material needs to be forked into a new pile. This moves the material that was on the outside toward the middle. Every three to four weeks, turn (remix) the pile again. The compost should be ready to use within three to four months.

The compost is ready to use when it is dark brown, crumbly, and earthy smelling. A layer of 1 to 2 inches (2.5 to 5 centimeters) can be mixed with the soil's surface. This is called mulch gardening. Mulch gardening makes it easier to control unwanted weeds. By composting at home, people can help protect the environment, save money, and improve the soil.

Source: USDA Natural Resources Conservation Service

ronment because it keeps home and yard types of organic garbage from taking up valuable space in the landfills—space that is quickly running out. According to the USDA Natural Resources Conservation Service, household organic wastes make up 20% to 30% of all household wastes. Processing your own compost and using it as fertilizer also reduces the need to use chemical fertilizers, which helps the environment.

CONSERVATION OF WATER RESOURCES—CURBING EROSION, SEDIMENTATION, AND RUNOFF

Soil and water conservation practices to help retain sediment and reduce runoff include structures such as berms (earthen diversions), sediment basins, drainage ditches, field drains, underground outlets, contour plowing and drip irrigation. Conservation practices also include grassed waterways, cover cropping, mulching, fencing, and offsite water on grazing lands.

The existence of sediment basins, water detention basins, and vegetative buffer strips at the edges of fields and waterways can help filter runoff and collect sediments and associated chemicals. Grassed waterways can prevent erosion, trap sediments, and use excess nutrients. Underground outlets can direct excess runoff from slopes to sediment basins. Berms can be used to direct runoff into natural channels or sediment basins. Cover cropping and contour cultivation can be used to reduce on-site erosion and runoff.

Water that moves away from crops can increase erosion and transport nutrients and pesticides away from crops and into surface or ground water where they can become pollutants. These situations can waste precious water resources and deplete aquifers and other sources of water.

For these reasons, the issue of water conservation is an important one. Many farmers have opted to use practices such as drip/micro-irrigation, automated timers or controls with moisture sensors, regular inspections and repairs of the irrigation system equipment, and increasing the uniformity in distribution of water.

Water conservation practices can also include capture of runoff and recycling of irrigation water to reduce water use. Capturing water runoff from winter rain and snow, and using it to irrigate their fields is another way farmers can conserve water resources.

BACKYARD CONSERVATION: URBAN REVITALIZATION

Just as farmers do on their farms, conservation practices on nonagricultural land can help increase food and shelter for birds and other wildlife, reduce sediment in waterways, conserve water and improve water quality, control soil erosion, beautify the landscape, and inspire a land stewardship outlook.

Urban revitalization is popular with inhabitants of cities and suburban areas. Many residents enjoy gardening, landscaping, and the pride of producing on their land, whether they grow fruits and vegetables or beautiful flower gardens. Many cities also strive to beautify the environment by creating large tracts of land devoted to parks, horticulture, and beautiful gardens.

Recycling Agricultural Wastes to Produce Hot Water

Composting is the time-honored process of converting agricultural or gardening wastes into fertilizer. During the composting process, an important by-product is heat. This production of heat, if tapped, can be used to supply hot water for a home. If the compost pile is large enough and produces enough heat, the heat can be captured by a simple heat exchanger. The heat exchanger can be a coil of flexible plastic pipe embedded in the interior of the compost heap.

Heat from the decomposition penetrates the pipe and heats the water, which is circulating inside. The cold water, initially put into the pipe, warms up while it is in the portion of the pipe within the compost heap. When a faucet is opened at the other end, hot water will emerge until the incoming cold water replaces the heated water. When the stored hot water is used up, repeating the process will regenerate it.

This appreciation of nature and the land is often referred to as "backyard conservation" and achieved by anyone who wants to conserve and improve natural resources on the land and help the environment.

Whether people have acres of land in the country, an average-sized suburban yard, or a tiny plot within the city, they can help protect the environment and beautify their surroundings. Backyard conservation provides habitat for birds and other wildlife, healthier soil, erosion control, water conservation, and nutrient management. The following conservation practices are popular and easy for almost anyone to accomplish.

Backyard Ponds and Wetlands

Backyard ponds are usually built where they can be seen from a deck or patio. A backyard pond does not need to be big—it can be as small as 3 to 4 feet (1 to 1.2 meters) wide. Landscaping around a pond provides shelter for wildlife. Ponds must be made with a protective liner in order to keep the water from seeping into the soil. Many people use pumps and filters in their ponds and build waterfalls on the side that cascade into the pool. They also put fish in the pond for additional habitat and aesthetic enjoyment. Fish also keep insect populations under control (a form of integrated pest management).

Plants can be used in the pond environment. A combination of emergent, submergent, and floating species can be used. Emergent plants have their roots in the water but their shoots above water. They are found on the margins of the pond. Examples of emergent plants are cattails and water lilies.

Submergent species remain underwater. They are often used as **oxygenators**. These plants remove carbon dioxide from the water and add oxygen. They also help keep the water clear.

Floating species are not anchored at all in the pond. Examples of floating species include duckweed, water lettuce, and water hyacinth. These plants also help keep the water clear by limiting the amount of sunlight that the algae receive and need to grow.

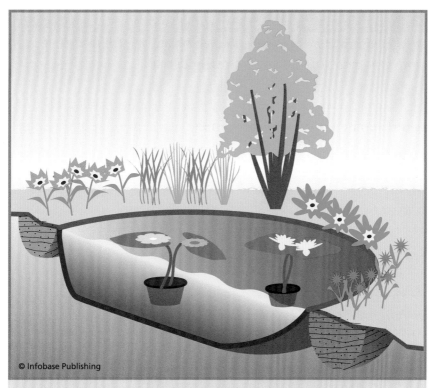

This illustration shows what a typical backyard pond might look like.

On a farm, a properly located and maintained pond can reduce gully erosion and improve water quality. Ponds provide a water source for livestock, waterfowl, and fish. They also store water for emergencies. Wildlife uses the ponds for water and habitat.

A mini-wetland in a backyard can provide many of the same benefits that natural wetlands offer. A mini-wetland can also replace the natural function of the land that was in place before the ground was developed and houses were built. Backyard wetlands are advantageous because they temporarily store, filter, and clean runoff water from the house and lawn. They also provide habitat for many forms of life, such as toads, frogs, salamanders, butterflies, bees, and birds. Fortunately, many wetland plants do not require standing water in

(Top) Planting a backyard garden is an excellent way to learn about conservation. *(Courtesy of USDA Natural Resources Conservation Service; photo by Lynn Betts)*

(Bottom) A backyard pond and wetland in Cantril, Iowa. Ponds are a rewarding way to practice conservation and provide habitat and biodiversity. *(Courtesy of USDA Natural Resources Conservation Service; photo by Lynn Betts)*

order to grow. Wetlands can be naturally built into a low or continually wet spot in the yard or an area can be converted into one.

A wetland is just an area where water covers the soil or keeps it saturated for at least two to three weeks during the growing season. It can be placed anywhere that water accumulates faster than it drains away. Wetlands grow grasses, cattails, and other marshy vegetation. How long the soil is kept wet at a time will determine which plants can grow there.

On the farm, wetlands filter chemicals, excess nutrients, and sediment from flowing water. Because of this, they protect streams and drinking water sources. They also provide wildlife habitat. Many farmers keep former natural wetlands in crop fields and pastures as fully functioning wetlands. Keeping these areas as wetlands provides ecological, economic, and aesthetic benefits. Farmers often enhance their wetlands with nesting structures for ducks and other birds, put in plants and seed to provide winter food and cover for wildlife, and establish native wildflowers.

Backyard Mulching

Mulching is one of the simplest and most beneficial practices used in a garden. As illustrated earlier on a farm setting, mulch is simply a protective layer of a material that is spread on top of the soil. Mulches can be organic, such as grass clippings, straw, or bark chips; they can also consist of inorganic materials, such as stones, brick chips, and plastic. Mulching is beneficial in backyard gardens for many reasons. It protects the soil from erosion, reduces soil compaction from heavy rains, and prevents weed growth. It also helps conserve soil moisture so the garden does not have to be watered as often. In addition, mulching helps the soil maintain a more even temperature.

Organic mulch improves the condition of the soil. When mulch decomposes in the soil, it provides the organic matter that helps keep the soil structure loose and aerated, not compacted. Because of this, plant roots grow better, and water infiltrates the soil better, allowing the soil to hold more water. Mulch is also a source of plant nutrients and provides a healthy environment for earthworms and other beneficial soil organisms.

As discussed earlier, farmers use mulch in several ways. When conservation tillage is practiced, it creates a natural mulch on the soil's surface. The mulch often consists of straw, bean stems, and corn stalks. The mulch also protects the soil against erosion. Research is showing that leaving crop residue helps keep carbon in the soil and reduces greenhouse gases.

Backyard Nutrient Management

Plants require many nutrients, even in backyard gardens. Nitrogen, phosphorus, and potassium are required in the largest amounts. Nitrogen is responsible for lush vegetation; phosphorus for flowering and fruiting of plants; and potassium to improve resistance to disease. In addition, calcium, magnesium, and sulfur are also very important. These six nutrients are referred to as macronutrients.

What Is the Difference Between Biodegradable and Renewable?

Biodegradable means that the material used in the production of something disintegrates and becomes compost—part of the natural environment. An example of something biodegradable is organic material, such as wood or leaves, which will decompose over time back into the environment. Renewable means that the material used in the production of something can be re-created any number of times without depleting the resource. Crops are considered a renewable resource because, through their seeds, they can be regenerated year after year (as long as conservation practices are maintained and the soil is kept healthy).

Something to think about: If soil is considered to be a nonrenewable resource (because it takes so long to form), can composting and adding the compost to the soil (soil augmentation) make it a renewable resource?

Soil also needs micronutrients—important nutrients required in only small amounts. These nutrients include zinc, iron, copper, and boron. The level of nutrients can be a delicate balancing act. While it is important for the soil to have them, they can be detrimental if they exist in too large of quantities. Not only can they harm plant growth, but they can also infiltrate and pollute groundwater or surface waters.

One way to manage nutrients in a backyard conservation environment is to use a soil testing kit. It allows for the testing and determination of concentrations of nutrients and soil pH levels so that the correct level of nutrients can be added. In this way, nutrients are not over applied and excess nutrients are not subsequently loaded into clean lakes or streams. Once the results of the soil test are known, nutrients—or other soil amendments, such as lime—can be added as needed. Compost can be added to provide the essential nutrients.

Farmers routinely test their soils to determine the nutrient status. Using the precision farming techniques previously described, nutrients can be added in specific amounts in specific areas of the field. Farmers can apply a variety of fertilizer materials, including livestock manure, commercial nitrogen, green manure crops, and crop rotations involving legumes.

Backyard Pest Management

Just as on farms, backyard gardens also have pest problems. Yard pests include weeds, insects, and diseases, such as fungi, bacteria, and viruses.

Insects can damage plants in many ways. They can chew plant leaves and flowers. Some, such as aphids, mealy bugs, and mites, can suck out plant juices; others cause damage by burrowing into stems, fruits, and leaves.

Planting resistant varieties of plants can prevent many pest problems, including disease. Rotating annual crops in a garden also prevents some diseases. Plants that have the correct amount of nutrients available in the soil are also more resistant to disease, because they are in a healthier environment. Mulching is effective against the spread of weeds.

Similar to farms, backyard conservation methods can include some form of integrated pest management, which relies on several techniques to manage pests without the excessive use of chemical controls. IPM can include monitoring plants, determining tolerable injury levels, and applying appropriate pest management. IPM does not treat the entire area with a chemical—it looks at specific areas that need control and applies them in only the effected areas, in the correct amounts, and at the correct time. Spot spraying is an example of this type of management. It is cost effective and limits damage to nontargeted species.

Management practices for weeds include hoeing, pulling, and mulching. Weeding is most important when plants are small. Well-established plants can often tolerate competition from weeds.

Disease management generally involves the removal of diseased plants. Diseased branches on trees can be pruned. Additives to soil are also available to reduce damage from some insects. Biological controls are also useful. Some insects are predators of pests and can help keep their populations under control.

Rotating crops to reduce disease and insect infestations accomplishes pest management of farms; growing tall grass hedges provides habitat for beneficial insects.

Farmers also monitor their fields for signs of pests in the early stages. When insect or weed populations reach an unacceptable level, control measures are started. When farmers do apply pesticides, using responsible conservation techniques, they are applied only to the land where the problems exist. Many farmers use IPM to control pests.

Backyard Terracing

Terraces are used in backyards that consist of steep slopes. Terraces can create several backyard mini-gardens to grow flowers and vegetables. Terraces prevent erosion by shortening a long slope into a series of level steps. This enables heavy rains to soak into the soil rather than creating runoff and contributing to soil erosion.

On a farm, terracing catches runoff water and enables it to soak into the ground. Excess water is then safely transported to the bottom of a hillside in a controlled way. Some terraces are covered with grass in order to provide erosion control as well as nesting areas for birds.

Backyard Tree Planting

When trees are planted in the backyard, they can provide valuable habitat for many types of wildlife. Trees can also help reduce home heating and cooling costs, help clean the air, and provide shelter from the wind.

On a farm, windbreaks and tree plantings slow the wind and provide habitat for wildlife. Trees can shelter livestock and crops. These play an important role in conservation practices. Trees in urban areas help prevent dust particles from adding to smog.

Backyard Water Conservation

Wise use of water for gardens and lawns helps to protect the environment and provides for optimum growing conditions. There are many practices available to promote backyard water conservation. Growing species of xerophytes (plants that can survive in dry conditions) is one way. Plants that use low amounts of water include Yucca, California poppy, blanket flower, moss rose, Juniper, sage, thyme, crocus, and primrose.

Other water conservation methods include using mulches and installing windbreaks to slow winds and help reduce evapotranspiration. Watering in the early morning is also a beneficial conservation practice. If watering is done before the sun is intense enough to cause evaporation, more water will be utilized directly by the plant. Another method some gardeners use is drip, or trickle irrigation—plastic tubing that supplies a slow, steady source of water from sprinkler heads suspended above the ground.

Backyard terracing is constructed on slopes. The steplike pattern keeps the ground level in order to prevent water erosion.

Native plants (plants that grow naturally in the area) are also important because they naturally use less water than nonnative species. Native species have evolved under local conditions and usually have well-developed mechanisms for surviving extremes in the weather.

On the farm, trickle irrigation is commonly used for high value crops, such as vegetables, grapes, and berries. High-efficiency irrigation systems for row crops use less energy to pump water. In addition, because they spray water downward, less water evaporates before it reaches the crop.

Wildlife Habitat

Habitat is a combination of food, water, shelter, and space that meets the needs of a species of wildlife. Even a small yard can be landscaped to attract birds, butterflies, small animals, and insects. Trees, shrubs, and other plants provide shelter and food for wildlife. Nesting boxes, feeders, and watering sites can be added to improve the habitat.

Wildlife habitat covers the horizontal dimension (the size of the yard) as well as a vertical component from the ground to the treetops. Different wildlife species live in the different vertical zones, enabling several habitats to exist in a backyard setting. Trees and shrubs are also important sources of food for wildlife. Birdhouses and shelters are easy to add to a backyard habitat to increase the wildlife that visits the area. Plant species that birds enjoy can be grown to encourage wildlife visits. Clean, fresh water is also critical in a backyard habitat. Birds, bats, butterflies, and other wildlife need a source of water. Water can be stored in a saucer, birdbath, or backyard pond.

On farms, private landowners provide most of the habitat for wildlife in the United States. They provide wildlife habitat on about 70% of the land. Farmers accomplish this by installing grasses, trees, shrubs, riparian buffer strips, ponds, wetlands, and other types of wildlife habitat. Some farmers even plant food plots especially suited for wildlife, or put up structures that geese, ducks, and other birds can use as protected nests. Some farmers plant food plots of corn, millet, or other grains that wildlife enjoy.

THE CRITICAL LINK BETWEEN PRIVATE LAND AND ECOSYSTEMS

Because 70% of the land in the United States is privately owned, it is not hard to understand why it is so important for landowners to be conservation minded. That does not just apply to those who farm the land—it applies to everybody. The same conservation methods apply whether someone lives on a farm, in a house in the suburbs with a backyard, or in the city. Everyone plays a part in keeping water safe and clean, and preventing pollution.

When private landowners care about conservation and ecosystems, and they strive to reduce, reuse, and recycle precious resources, they are taking a responsible and active role in land stewardship—and land stewardship is the key to a successful agricultural future.

CHAPTER

9

CONCLUSION: FUTURE ISSUES AND LAND STEWARDSHIP

This chapter discusses technology for the future, ongoing agricultural research, biosecurity for agriculture, farmland preservation, land stewardship, and how the U.S. space program is currently using agriculture. It is predicted that by the year 2030 the world's population will reach 8 billion, and 10 billion by 2050. In order to feed that many people and eliminate hunger, farmers must either double the amount of land they farm or become much more efficient. Today, farmers worldwide farm enough land to equal a landmass the size of South America. If farmers cannot become more productive, scientists predict that by 2050 farmers will have to farm enough land to equal a landmass the size of both North and South America.

Agricultural technology and the ability to provide enough food for people is a worldwide concern. It is estimated that more than 800 million people today do not have enough food. Malnutrition is a serious problem—more than 6 million deaths of children under 5 years old occur each year because of this serious issue. Growing enough staple crops—such as wheat, rice, corn, and potatoes—without increasing the amount of land farmed will require a substantial increase in the food yield per acre.

One possibility that scientists are looking at to accomplish this is agricultural biotechnology—the manipulation, through genetic engineering, of living organisms to produce commodities like pest resistant crops and stronger agricultural products. An example of a genetically engineered crop is Roundup Ready Corn, developed by Monsanto. This corn is a genetically engineered hybrid that is resistant to Roundup (a widely used grass herbicide). This corn allows farmers to avoid using many of the herbicides that growers of other types of corn have to use. Herbicide-resistant crops are just one example of agricultural biotechnology. Biotechnology is also being used to develop crops with enhanced yields, built-in insect resistance, and other special traits, such as improved fiber cotton and improved protein corn, or corn that contains biodegradable plastic polymers.

Farmers have been battling pests in their fields for centuries. They have used everything from conventional plant-breeding techniques to chemicals, such as pesticides and herbicides. Now scientists are using advanced molecular biology as a tool to improve plants by inserting genes that enable them to naturally be more resistant to pests.

Although traditional plant breeding practices have existed and been used for many years, scientists are now able to pinpoint specific beneficial genes from one species and transfer those genes into another crop's genetics so that it can benefit from them, as well.

For many countries, a major challenge for sustainable development will be finding ways to link conservation and biotechnology to increase agricultural production on less land, with lower pesticide use. Some countries, such as Kenya, have already used biotechnology to increase production of bananas, potatoes, and sugarcane. So far today, most genetically modified technology has been developed primarily for large-scale agriculture in the industrialized world in order to make certain crops more resistant to certain insects or viruses. Currently, almost 100 million acres of genetically modified crops have been grown worldwide. While many people favor scientific advances, others have concerns about genetically modified crops. There has been no evidence of human health problems associated specifically with these crops or food products, but some people are concerned about the potential for these crops to cause allergic reactions or produce toxic compounds.

The USDA leads the world in basic and applied research, as it looks for ways to solve the problems challenging America's food and fiber production; and for ways to improve food supply, safety, and quality. The USDA has identified five major agricultural challenges in the next decade:

1. Maintaining a competitive agricultural system in global trade
2. Balancing agricultural production and the environment
3. Providing a safe and secure food supply for everyone
4. Maintaining a healthy, well-nourished population
5. Increasing economic opportunities and improving the quality of life for all Americans

There are four USDA agencies that strive to make these things happen through research and education: the Agricultural Research Service (ARS), the Cooperative State Research, Education, and Extension Service (CSREES), the Economic Research Service (ERS), and the National Agricultural Statistics Service (NASS).

USDA research advances in agricultural biotechnology help improve crop quality and yields. They are also behind integrated pest management—using natural techniques to control pests instead of chemical pesticides—in order to reduce health risks and protect natural resources. One product that the USDA has developed is a substance called Z-trim, which can be used in a number of food products as a fat replacement that tastes good.

The USDA accomplishes much of its research and testing through partnerships with individual state agricultural experiment stations based at various universities. It is through these important connections that cutting-edge technologies and new products have been developed. USDA research also focuses on practical education that Americans can use in dealing with critical issues that affect their lives and the nation's future by linking research, science, and technology to the needs of the people. It offers programs on food safety, health care concerns, water quality, conservation of natural resources, sustainable agriculture, nutrition programs, and 4-H Club activities.

AGRICULTURE AND SCIENCE FOR THE TWENTY-FIRST CENTURY

Although there is plenty of food in the world, a lot of it is in the wrong place—most of the food exists only in developed countries (like the United States). In order to feed all the people in the world, farmers have to find more efficient ways of farming.

Farming is hard work. It is also a science. Farmers benefit from the research and discoveries of scientists. Scientists, over the years, have helped farmers by breeding better livestock, improving farming equipment and machinery, creating more effective fertilizers, and crossbreeding crops in order to improve them. Scientists conduct their research in laboratories, factories, universities, and on farms. What is eaten and how farming is done in the future depends largely on science. It also depends on governments in different parts of the world.

Plant breeders are constantly finding new crops developed to suit all types of soil and climate. Research into new varieties of crops is going on all over the world. This type of science is called crossbreeding—two different crops can be combined in order to produce a new type of crop that has characteristics of both the parent crops. This process produces new types of food. It also allows the good traits from two different crops to be combined to form better and much stronger offspring. This can make crops more resistant to hot climates, cold climates, dry climates, poor soils, insects, and many other things.

As advances are made in communication, information, and transportation technologies, their effect has been to "shrink" the globe, making goods and services more readily available to everyone on a worldwide basis. The effects of this also affect food and agriculture.

State-of-the-art scientific techniques now exist to study the need for nutrients over the entire human life cycle. Unraveling the human genome may spur the development methods to identify the nutritional needs of individuals. Upcoming technological advances in understanding the plant and animal genome sequences provide a way to improve not only nutritional needs, but also process-related and environmental needs. Research to identify and link at-risk populations to scientific discoveries promises advancements in reducing malnutrition and obesity.

With the advent of cutting-edge research and new technology, discoveries are being made in the production of agriculture, food safety, and nutrition. These discoveries are then passed on to farmers, ranchers, consumers, food processors, and others who can use them.

AGRICULTURAL RESEARCH AND HOW IT IMPROVES OUR DAILY LIVES

The Agricultural Research Service (ARS) is the principal research agency of the USDA. ARS research has contributed to crop yields and more environmentally friendly farming techniques. ARS research goes much further than the farm, however. It also focuses on human health and other important related issues.

Agricultural research has been in place and benefiting society for many years. One of agriculture's greatest gifts to modern medicine was the invention of penicillin. In 1928, Alexander Fleming, a Scottish bacteriologist, discovered a mold with bacteria-killing powers so incredible, it was effective even when diluted 800 times. The nontoxic mold turned out to have a high therapeutic value.

Efforts to product it in large amounts kept failing, however. Then, in 1941, two British scientists brought the mold to the United States for further research. They got together with scientists at the Agricultural Research Service and discovered the secret was corn steep liquor— which was familiar to agricultural researchers as a byproduct of the wet-corn milling process. They continued to experiment with it and eventually developed a superior strain of penicillin, found on a moldy cantaloupe in a garbage can. When the new strain was made available to drug companies, production skyrocketed. Fortunately for soldiers in World War II, penicillin was available to treat the Allied soldiers.

Agricultural research has continued over the years. The ARS recently developed a fat substitute called Oatrim. This technology not only helps farmers by finding another use for oats, it also allows processors to produce better tasting low-fat foods. Consumers benefit from a health standpoint because this technology lowers the bad type of cholesterol without decreasing the good type of cholesterol. It also improves glucose tolerance.

The ARS also develops industrial products, such as printing ink made from soybeans and other crops. This is beneficial to the environment because the ink does not have to be made from a petroleum product. Unlike petroleum, soybeans are a renewable resource.

The ARS conducts research on problems that require long-term commitment of resources. Such research includes discovering ways to protect crops and livestock from pests and diseases, making agricultural commodities better and safer, and making the best use of natural resources. The ARS also developed biodegradable lubricants made from vegetable oil—which helps decrease the use of expensive petroleum—and improved varieties of cotton **germplasm**, which leads to decreased pesticide use.

Each year, dozens of improved products and new varieties of fruits, nuts, and vegetables are introduced from the laboratories and greenhouses of the ARS. Other notable achievements of the ARS include the following:

- Fresh apples: Apples in the grocery store may have been stored for up to nine months, but they still remain crisp because of the controlled-atmosphere-storage method invented by the ARS. They have also developed new non-chemical biocontrols to harness naturally occurring yeasts and bacteria and use them to fight apples' enemies. They have even developed a "bashless" bagging-packaging system that allows wholesalers to ship the fruit without bruising.

- Onions, carrots, garlic, and cucumbers: ARS research has developed methods to make these foods taste better and contain more nutrients. They also yield more crops and more readily resist disease. The ARS has also developed a carrot that is healthier than ever. Today's carrots contain twice the beta-carotene as carrots did 30 years ago.
- Single-serve lettuce: ARS plant breeders devised an iceberg mini-lettuce that makes just enough salad for one person to eat at one sitting.
- Peaches: The ARS has developed peaches that can now be grown in cooler northern climates. A laboratory technique called embryo culture has been very helpful in creating new peach varieties. It has developed a peach that is resistant to a disease called Peach Tree Short Life as well as a bacterial control that prevents brown rot on the fruit.
- Pecans: The ARS conducts the world's only pecan-breeding program. It has developed a pecan that is both insect- and disease-resistant, produces larger nuts, and grows in greater quantities.
- Berries: These sweet fruits are fragile and can be difficult to grow. They usually have brief growing seasons and are highly vulnerable to insects and disease. The ARS has developed strawberries that resist a disease called red stele, berries that ripen earlier, and berries that bear fruit from spring until well into the fall. It has also developed blueberries that ripen earlier, and the first genetic thornless blackberries.
- Peanuts: ARS scientists have found ways to improve peanut flavor and quality. They have also discovered ways

to extend the shelf life of peanut products, as well as remove part of the oil from the peanut without serious loss of flavor, in order to lower the fat content.

- Grain: Thanks to the ARS, at the touch of a few buttons, a grower can get customized advice on diseases to watch out for and treatments that are appropriate to specific conditions.
- Freezer-friendly frozen food: When frozen food was first introduced years ago, people complained about the funny color, lack of taste, and the cardboard texture. People also worried about the loss of nutrients and possible bacterial contamination during processing and storage. In response to this, the ARS developed the Time-Temperature Tolerance Project. Through research and testing, scientists developed new ways to make frozen food much better. Researchers also found that rapid freezing of berries and beans with liquid nitrogen created better products. The ARS improved the consistency of frozen gravies and sauces. Changing from rice flour to wheat flour improved the consistency of these food items. Scientists also developed dehydrofreezing, a process in which fruits and vegetables are partially dehydrated before freezing in order to cut their weight in half. Its main use today is in freezing pieces of potatoes and apples.
- Citrus fruit: More than 70% of all citrus fruit grown in the United States are varieties developed by the ARS citrus breeding program. This program has increased the yield, increased disease resistance, and created a longer shelf life. After 20 years of experimenting, the ARS also developed citrus that can withstand periodic cold snaps—good news for citrus farmers.
- Cheese: The ARS is constantly helping cheese producers to develop more effective and reliable processing methods. Scientists have also developed a chemical test that helps cheese makers ensure that their cheeses are properly aged

for sale. They have developed a new method to produce a mozzarella cheese that contains only 10% fat (regular mozzarella contains 23% fat).

- Lactose-free dairy products: The ARS developed the lactose-free dairy products that help people who have trouble digesting lactose. Scientists accomplished this by altering a bacterium used to make cheese and yogurt, which   produces an enzyme that breaks down milk's lactose, keeping consumers from getting an upset stomach.

- Grapes: ARS scientists continually experiment with different varieties of grapes to produce better-tasting grapes. The ARS laboratory developed America's most popular red seedless grape. Scientists have also developed a delicious new black seedless grape.

- Potatoes: ARS research has developed new, improved potato varieties, including ones that produce potato chips with lower fat content than any other. The ARS was also responsible for the invention of instant potato flakes, which were developed in 1954 to help use up surplus potatoes. Today, about 400 million pounds of potato flakes are produced each year in the United States.

- Poultry: The ARS is responsible for breeding turkeys that contain more white meat. Their scientific innovations have also made breeding and raising turkeys easier and more efficient for producers. Keeping dangerous microorganisms out of poultry is an ARS goal. Through research, it is now possible to vaccinate hatching eggs against coccidiosis—a chicken disease that costs producers about $300 million each year. ARS scientists have also developed a similar method for injecting 'good' bacteria into incubating eggs to combat salmonella, which has made poultry safer for consumers.

- Beef: Research has been conducted on diseases such as Brucellosis, shipping fever, and bovine tuberculosis.

The research has resulted in many new animal medicines and programs to prevent disease transmission. Rangeland management practices have also been developed to match cattle populations to available forage, and grasses have been bred to offer top nutrient value while growing harmoniously alongside wild species.

- Sugar: ARS sugarcane research has developed 86 new varieties of sugarcane. These new varieties include high-yielding cane and other varieties that are more resistant to diseases, such as sugarcane mosaic virus, eye spot, smut, rust, ratoon stunting, and leaf scald. Some varieties have been bred to fend off insects. Scientists also developed two processes for making specialized sugars for the candy industry. One—turbinado sugar—is made directly from the cane juice during harvest without refinement. The other product is a sugar even whiter and purer than turbinado, which is used in pale-colored candies, like mints.

- Cotton: The ARS is improving cotton all the time. It was ARS scientists who conducted the initial work on flame-retardant finishes. They were first used in military combat clothing, firemen's uniforms, and hospital linens. Today, they are used in many different products, including children's pajamas.

- Biodegradable cutlery: To help with the problem of landfills that are getting overcrowded, the ARS has developed biodegradable knives, forks, and spoons made from a starch-polyester material to help lower the amount of petroleum-based plastics that currently take up about 25% of the volume of landfills. Scientists are also experimenting with these starch-polyesters to produce plastic bags and wraps.

- Tree-free paper: The ARS is working with a fast-growing plant called *kenaf*, which has shown promise as an alternative to wood pulp for papermaking.

Technician Christine Berry checks on futuristic peach and apple "orchards." Each dish holds tiny experimental trees grown from lab-cultured cells, to which researchers have added new genes. *(Courtesy of the Agricultural Research Service; photo by Scott Bauer)*

The application of research to science is a good investment. Not only does research make significant improvements to our food supply, but Americans also have a reliable and affordable supply of fresh and processed food at their disposal. In terms of costs, Americans pay much less for food than the citizens of other countries do.

NEW TECHNOLOGY AND DEVELOPMENTS

Spurred on by past successful experiments and improvements, scientists are continually creating new developments and technologies from agricultural research. The Agricultural Research Service has identified the following as promising future technologies.

Bovine Genome Sequencing Project

The National Human Genome Research Institute, the USDA, and other agencies in the United States and other countries are working on mapping the complete genome for cattle. They believe it will benefit human health and agriculture by eliminating hunger, improving nutrition, and reducing agriculture's impact on the environment. Benefits will be recognized in the world's health and world's food supplies. The bovine genome is similar in size to the genomes of humans and other mammals—it has about 3 billion base pairs. In addition to its potential for improving dairy and meat products and enhancing food safety, adding the genomic sequence of the cow to the growing list of sequenced animal genomes will help researchers learn more about the human genome. Understanding the genome will also help scientists combat disastrous diseases, such as mad cow disease.

Spinach Power

Scientists at the Massachusetts Institute of Technology are experimenting with spinach and its ability to convert sunlight to energy into developing a solid-state electronic device that may eventually be able to power laptops and cell phones. The secret behind the device is a protein complex derived from spinach chloroplasts. They are so tiny that about 100,000 of them could fit on the head of a pin, making them one of the smallest electronic circuits. Spinach plants make good candidates for this technology because they are very efficient, producing a large amount of energy relative to their size and weight.

Soy-based Elevator Fluid

A new innovation is being used on the Statue of Liberty's elevators. They now run on a biodegradable hydraulic fluid made from soy oil. The National Park Service (NPS) is using the new soy oil instead of traditional oil because soy is a renewable resource that is non-polluting. The fluid is a product of the ARS and was developed with many environmental attributes in mind: it breaks down readily in the environment in case there is a leak; it comes from a renewable resource; it is economical to produce and nonpolluting; and it is safe and performs well (it is stable and flame resistant).

Although other vegetable oils will also work, soy oil was selected because of its low cost, chemical versatility, and renewability. Today, soy is the nation's leading source of food-grade oil. During tests against mineral-based oils, soy proved better able to lubricate and more biodegradable. Scientists hope more innovations involving soy and other oilseed crops will take place in order to reduce the demand for petroleum-based products.

Biodiversity and Seed Banking

The ARS operates its own network of 'banks' that make up the National Plant Germplasm System. Consisting of 20 repositories and support units, they hold germplasm for scientists to study, breeders to grow, and land managers to use. The bank is a gold mine of plant species, with more than 82,000 plant samples in the seed collection.

The ARS is banking seeds because it wants to maintain genetic diversity in plants and animals collected from around the world. Seeds are dried, cleaned, and packaged before being frozen. Seeds are stored at 0° to −238° F (−18° to −150° C). They are cooled by liquid nitrogen because it slows deterioration and gives seeds a longer lifespan. Seeds that have short life spans, or are very valuable, are cooled to these temperatures for safekeeping.

By maintaining this supply of seeds, it is possible for plant varieties used in the past in similar environmental conditions to be used now or in the future, as conditions change. Growing conditions vary from year to year, pests migrate, and seasons vary from wet to dry. Each plant variety thrives in specific conditions; by banking a supply of the seeds, the plants will be available when and where they are needed.

As science expands its knowledge and ability, these seeds are preserved so that they can be used for research. Most crops grown in the United States actually originated from other countries. Immigrants brought them here from their native countries. These, and the native plants, are stored for safe keeping until they are needed. One extremely important application for plants is in medical research. Many plants are used to produce medicines. One plant, for example, is showing promise in helping breast cancer patients.

This research is extremely valuable. The seed bank gives scientists a way to understand why certain varieties are able to survive under difficult conditions. Understanding a plant's molecular makeup is the first step in knowing what makes a plant resistant to disease or pests, and how well it thrives in different environments.

Bug Detectors

The ARS has developed a specialized microphone that can be put in the pots of nursery crops to detect the presence of black vine weevils. The person doing the listening wears headphones and places a wandlike device on a very large nail that has been placed in the root ball of the plant. Another handheld component then amplifies and measures the sounds. The weevil makes a distinctive clicking noise as its body vibrates off the soil. The portable listening device is efficient enough to test 15 to 25 pots per hour. Scientists believe this new device will revolutionize the detection of root-feeding pests like the weevil.

Corn Ethanol

Corn can be made into ethanol—a source of environmentally friendly, renewable fuel. Ethanol production in the United States grew from 175 million gallons (more than 6.62 million liters) in 1980 to a record 2.8 billion gallons (10.6 billion liters) in 2003. The increased demand for ethanol has created a significant new market for corn. Currently, almost 10% of the U.S. corn crop is used to make fuel ethanol, which is good for America's farmers. Ethanol is also good for the environment because its use reduces greenhouse gas emissions. Scientists are developing new ways to reduce the costs of producing this important fuel and other corn products. They are also creating computer models to help researchers and ethanol producers estimate how different techniques will affect the cost to produce it. Computer models can estimate the cost per gallon to produce ethanol using various processes.

GIS for Agriculture

Geographic Information Systems (GIS) are being used in many aspects of science today. Their ability to store spatial information and use statistical models to produce interactive maps that can be used in many agricultural applications makes them valuable technology; and more applications are being discovered all the time. For example, in precision agriculture, maps can be created to portray the different fertility regions in a crop field so that, when fertilizer is applied, areas that need more get more; and areas that need less, get less. Environmentally this is a much better approach than the old one-size-fits-all technique.

Another advantage to GIS is that data can be mapped and analyzed at different scales—whether at the subfield level analyzing crop yield information or internationally assisting governments with commodity subsidy programs. Not only can GIS analyze data quickly, they can analyze different types of data at the same time and identify relationships, potential conflicts, and compatibilities between different environmental questions.

Cows and Satellites

Farmers are now tracking cattle using satellites. By using Global Positioning System (GPS) technology, special GPS receiver collars can be attached to cows so that their movements and locations can be monitored throughout the day. There are 24 to 30 satellites in orbit around the Earth to constantly supply locational data.

Researchers want to know why cattle travel where they do. A better understanding of grazing behavior will allow managers to distribute cattle more effectively. Livestock distribution is a major issue for ranchers, and GPS technology is the first tool to allow researchers to learn why cattle graze where they do.

Using satellites and GPS, researchers can determine within a few meters where a cow was and at what time it was there. Not only can the GPS units tell where the cattle are, they can detect head movement so that researchers know when cattle eat and sleep.

Once scientists collect the GPS data, the information is put in a computer and used in a GIS system. Computer predictive models can be created to predict where cattle will roam and forage. They can also model the effect that fences, trails, water, and prescribed burns will have on grazing.

Ducks and Rice

Japanese farmers have had success combining ducks and rice fields. Experiments have shown that the birds eat the weeds and pests that plague rice fields. The ducks' droppings also serve as fertilizer to nourish the rice, which then creates higher crop yields. Unexpected symbiotic relationships such as this may play a larger role in agriculture in the future.

BIOSECURITY FOR AGRICULTURE

Governments play a critical role in providing for the availability of food to be grown, imported, and exported around the world. One of our nation's biggest concerns since the terrorist attacks on September 11, 2001, is biosecurity. This concern includes not only defending the nation from direct attacks to people, but also from attacks that attempt to disrupt America's ability to feed itself and the world. A single animal or plant disease outbreak not quickly controlled could drastically affect our ability to keep our animals and plants healthy. It could also shake consumer confidence in a food supply perceived to have been safe.

In response, the United States government has increased funding to help ensure a safe food supply. The agricultural budget not only provides funds to protect America's food supply and agricultural systems, but also improves nutrition and health, conserves and enhances our natural resources, and provides business opportunities for farmers.

Efforts are being directed toward the ability to rapidly identify and characterize a bioterrorist attack. The government is working on improving surveillance capabilities in areas such as human health, food, agriculture, and the environment. Specific programs developed to accomplish these goals include activities such as increasing the monitoring of pests and diseases in plants and animals; research on emerging animal diseases; increasing the availability of vaccines; tracking disease agents of plants; and establishing a federal-state monitoring network in all 50 states.

In order to achieve these goals, the USDA is currently working with other government agencies, such as the Animal and Plant Health Inspection Service, the Food Safety Inspection Service, the Office of the Inspector General, the Centers for Disease Control and Prevention, and the Department of Homeland Security.

Several conservation programs for the environmental protection of natural resources have also been put in place, including:

- Wetlands Reserve Program
- Farm and Ranch Land Protection Program
- Grassland Reserve Program
- Ground and Surface Water Conservation Program
- Wildlife Habitat Incentives Program
- Conservation Security Program

The government is also providing record-level funding for domestic food-assistance programs that focus on nutrition and fighting hunger. The government has a strong commitment to providing economic opportunities for American farmers by increasing opportunities for foreign trade.

The productivity of American farmers has allowed the United States to lead the world in global food aid. The United States is highly involved in food-assistance programs, such as the McGovern-Dole International Food for Education and Child Nutrition Program.

AGRICULTURE IN SPACE

Agriculture may seem like something that would only be found on Earth, but that is not the case. Today, scientists living and working on the International Space Station are studying agriculture and the effects that outer space has on it.

In order for space exploration to exist, astronauts must have a way to feed themselves—especially if they spend months in space. They also must make sure that their limited resources—such as oxygen, water, and soil—are preserved and well managed. These issues are critical to their survival.

Space agricultural research also affects agriculture on Earth, because it has the potential to improve the ways farmers grow and process foods here. Some of the space-based research currently being conducted includes testing new ways to package and preserve food for future space missions, as well as for food on Earth; exploring ways to use space technology in order to more effectively fertilize plants on Earth; developing technologies to efficiently use and recycle water; and planting specialized crops that can grow in microgravity.

If astronauts can learn to grow, harvest, and store food in space, they will be able to explore planets like Mars and places even further away—places that would require them to be away from Earth for months or years. Astronauts are experimenting with new ways to grow seeds, conserve soil resources, and even work with new kinds of food. Space agriculture also presents extraordinary possibilities for increasing crop yield—discoveries that will help people everywhere.

Agricultural research in space is not a new concept. Research began during the early days of space exploration. For example, the Apollo astronauts that landed on the Moon in 1969 brought lunar soil back to Earth, where scientists attempted to grow seeds in it. As space exploration has become more advanced and sophisticated, so has agricultural research. The National Aeronautics and Space Administration (NASA) is interested in creating bioregenerative life support systems that can support human and plant life forever.

Bioregenerative life-support systems perform all the basic functions of a life-support system. Its natural cycle allows it to continue regenerating itself. The Earth is a perfect example of a regenerative system with natural cycles. The Earth system continually provides food, water, and air as the important life cycles discussed in Chapter 3 described. In space, plants provide food, carbon dioxide uptake, oxygen generation, and water purification.

There are several challenges for space-based agriculture, however. The lack of gravity in outer space presents some unique dilemmas, because it is the gravity on Earth that helps plants establish strong rooting. Available sunlight and nutrients are another issue, as are insects for cross-pollination, controlled climate, and the availability of clean water.

Plants and people work well together in a closed system like this, however. Humans breathe air and produce carbon monoxide—plants consume the carbon monoxide and give off oxygen.

On Earth, energy is in the form of sunlight, but in space, availability of sunlight is not constant like it is on Earth. In space, the source of energy is provided in the form of light. Specifically, the same light emitting diodes (LEDs) that are used on Earth in many electronics. LEDs are used because they give light in the specific frequencies that plants need in order for photosynthesis to take place. LEDs are also more energy efficient that other light sources.

Clean water is created from the self-sustaining natural cleaning and filtration systems created in the space life-support systems. Gravity is generated through microgravity systems developed for long-term trips.

Space-based research is already helping Earth-based agriculture. Studies are being conducted involving custom crops that withstand hostile conditions, resist disease, and require less space to grow. Scientists believe that if food production can be sustained in space then it will be possible for human life to be established anywhere in the universe. For space exploration involving many months, the best system for growing crops is with controlled environment agriculture. Plants are grown in growth chambers controlled by computers, where all of the environmental factors can be controlled, such as nutrients, light, humidity, and temperature. A favored growth method is hydroponics; water transpired by the plants can also be collected and used as drinking water by the astronauts.

Research is also being conducted on controlling the greenhouse environment; light and nutrients are supplied at specific times when optimal conditions in the plants themselves exist. Someday scientists plan to have space agriculture operated by automated or robotic crop production systems. One thing scientists have discovered is that plants grown in a controlled environment usually produce more food than plants in the field. This is because it is a less stressful environment for plants—temperature, humidity, light, water, and nutrients are all tailored to the plant's individual needs.

Special seeds called super-dwarf seeds have also been developed for use in outer space. Different varieties have been developed, such as wheat, rice, tomatoes, soybeans, peas, and peppers. These crops are genetically engineered to only grow to short heights so that they can be grown on shelves. One version of the wheat—called Apogee wheat—developed by researchers at Utah State University, took a decade to develop and is half the height of normal wheat. It grows about 12 inches (30.5 centimeters) tall. It also has fewer branches and smaller leaves than normal wheat, and plants grow closer together. Super-dwarf seeds produce high yields (up to three times higher), which also makes them an attractive solution to growing food in space.

Plants may also have a future place on Mars. Researchers have developed a genetically altered mustard plant that glows when it is stressed. Scientists see testing this plant as the first step toward human colonization of Mars. Scientists at the University of Florida were able to splice a fluorescent gene from a jellyfish into a mustard plant. They believe that adverse conditions—such as disease or lack of water—will trigger the plant to glow. By studying these effects, it may be possible to discover how to sustain plant and human life on Mars. Researchers want NASA to test the fluorescent plants on a mission to Mars in 2007. One version of the plant will glow green in soil that contains heavy metals. Another will be blue if the soil contains too much peroxide. Earth scientists will be able to monitor the plants' reactions via camera images.

FARMLAND PRESERVATION

Conversion of farmland to urban uses currently involves less than 0.1% of U.S. farmland per year, but local farm losses continue to cause concern and increase public support for farmland protection. The Earth only has a set amount of arable land. In order to be able to feed the world, it is important that valuable arable land be maintained.

Several solutions have been put into motion: farmland zoning (where land is designated for agricultural applications only), preferential tax assessments (tax breaks for owners of agricultural land), the formation of agricultural districts, passage of right-to-farm laws, and purchase-of-development rights (programs that actually pay farmers to give up their rights to develop their land).

Many people see the value in maintaining farmland and improving rural amenities, such as establishing open space, protecting scenic views, supporting wildlife habitat, and maintaining the land's rural character. Farmland provides unique and valuable qualities to life that are worth protecting, and in doing so, creates an environment for long-term land stewardship.

LAND STEWARDSHIP—A LONG-TERM COMMITMENT

As illustrated throughout this book, there are many critical facets involved in creating successful agriculture. From practical experience, farmers have gained knowledge about how to properly care for the land. With conservation in mind, farmers have worked hard to maintain and protect the fertility of their fields. Through their hard work, perseverance, dedication, and commitment, they have created the world's highest quality, and most reliable, source of food.

As populations increase and urban areas continue to encroach upon rural areas, a struggle sometimes occurs to maintain a healthy, well-balanced environment. That responsibility is not just for those that farm the land—it is for everyone. Everyone is somebody's neighbor, and everyone's actions have the potential to hurt or help the land. People can practice responsible conservation techniques in their own backyards. Everyone can do their part to promote water quality and biodiversity. Our responsible land management practices can benefit the environment by controlling erosion and the fertility of the soil. Our willingness to recycle, reduce, and reuse will help protect the environment now and for generations to come. In order to conserve our resources and promote land stewardship, people must realize it is a long-term commitment. Actions that are taken now can affect the environment for future generations. Everyone has a role in maintaining healthy ecosystems.

1700s   Northern U.S. farmers produce a variety of crops and livestock, sometimes supplemented by craftwork; Southern U.S. plantation agriculture concentrates on export crops. Tobacco is the chief cash crop of the South; oxen and horses are used to power crude wooden plows; all sowing is done by hand, cultivating by hoe, hay and grain cutting with sickle, and threshing with flail; transportation is by water, on trails, or through wilderness; colonies export tobacco, rice, grain, and meat products.

1805   Cotton begins to replace tobacco as the chief southern cash crop.

1813   First publicized use of fertilizers.

1815   Competition with western farm areas begins to force New England farmers out of wheat and meat production and into trucking, and dairy and tobacco production.

1819   Jethro Wood patents the iron plow with interchangeable parts.

1830   First steam-powered plowing; cotton becomes the most important cash crop in the Old South.

1836   First successful combine harvester is developed; U.S. Patent Office collects agricultural information and distributes seeds.

1837   John Deere and Leonard Andrus begin manufacturing steel plows; practical threshing machine is patented.

1840s   Factory-made agricultural machinery increases farmers' need for cash and encourages commercial farming; New York, Pennsylvania, and Ohio are the chief wheat states; 3,000 miles (4,828 km) of railroad track are constructed.

1841	Practical grain drill is patented.
1842	First grain elevator is built in Buffalo, New York.
1843	Sir John Lawes founds the commercial fertilizer industry by developing a process for making superphosphate.
1844	Practical mowing machine is patented.
1847	Irrigation begins in Utah.
1849	Mixed chemical fertilizers are sold commercially.
1850s	Major rail trunk lines from eastern cities cross the Appalachian Mountains; steam and clipper ships improve overseas transportation.
1854	Self-governing windmill is perfected.
1856	Two-horse straddle-row cultivator is patented.
1858	Mason jars are invented and used for home canning.
1860s	Cotton Belt begins to move westward; Corn Belt begins stabilizing in its present area.
1860	30,000 miles (48,278 km) of railroad are completed.
1862	U.S. Department of Agriculture (USDA) is created (without cabinet status).
1862–1875	Change from hand power to horses characterizes the first American agricultural revolution.
1866	Cattle boom accelerates settlement of Great Plains; range wars develop between farmers and ranchers.
1870s	Refrigerator cars are introduced, increasing national markets for fruits and vegetables.
1874	Glidden barbed wire is patented; fencing of rangeland ends era of unrestricted, open-range grazing; grasshopper plagues in the western U.S.
1877	U.S. Entomological Commission is established for work on grasshopper control.

1880 160,500 miles (258,288 km) of railroad are completed.

1881 Hybridized corn is produced.

1885 Texas becomes the chief cotton state.

1886 Blizzards, following drought and overgrazing, are disastrous to northern Great Plains cattle industry.

1888 The first long-haul shipment of a refrigerated freight car was made from California to New York.

1889 Bureau of Animal Industry discovers carrier of tick fever; USDA is raised to cabinet status.

1890s Increases in land under cultivation and number of immigrants becoming farmers boost agricultural output; agriculture becomes increasingly mechanized and commercialized.

1892 First successful gasoline tractor is developed by John Froelich.

1894 Division of Agricultural Soils is established in the USDA.

1899 Soil survey program begins with congressional authorization for mapping of tobacco lands.

1906 Pure Food and Drug Act is established: Meat Inspection Act is established.

1909–1920 Dryland farming boom on the Great Plains; extensive experimental work to breed disease-resistant varieties of plants, improve plant yield and quality, and increase productivity of farm animals.

1913 First trucks are used on farms in the United States; USDA's Office of Markets is established to promote farm marketing.

1916 Federal Farm Loan Act; 254,000 miles (402,317 km) of railroad are completed; Rural Post Roads Act begins regular federal subsidies for road building.

1917	Food Control and Production Acts is established.
1918	Airplanes are first used on farms for spraying poison on cotton fields.
1920s	Truckers begin to capture trade in perishables and dairy products.
1921–1922	Tariff acts raise rates for agricultural and other imports.
1921–1940	Long-term agricultural depression.
1929	Soil conservation experiment stations are authorized.
1932–1936	Drought and dust-bowl conditions develop.
1933	Soil Erosion Service is created in the Department of the Interior.
1934	Taylor Grazing Act is established.
1935	Soil Conservation Service is created in the USDA.
1937	Arkansas becomes the first state to enact the Standard State Soil Conservation Districts Law.
1940s	Many former southern sharecroppers migrate to war-related jobs in cities.
1945	Beginning of intensive farming of pigs, poultry, and milk; Food and Agriculture Organization of the United Nations is established.
1946	National School Lunch Act established; International Emergency Food Council is established.
1949	International Wheat Program is established.
1950s	Trucks and barges compete successfully for agricultural products as railroad rates climb.
1950	Large agricultural surpluses.
1954	Food for Peace Act is established; the number of tractors on farms exceeds the number of horses and mules for the first time.

1956 Great Plains Conservation Program is created to help protect the drought-prone Great Plains against wind erosion; Soil Bank Program is authorized.

1957 Poultry Inspection Act is established.

1959 Mechanical tomato harvester is developed.

1960s Financial condition of northeastern railroads deteriorates; rail abandonment accelerates; agricultural shipments by all-cargo planes increase.

1960 Hybrid corn seed is planted on 96% of the corn acreage.

1964 Food Stamp Act is established.

1966 Child Nutrition Act is established.

1970 National Environmental Policy Act is enacted to require assessment of impacts of federal actions on the environment; no-tillage agriculture is popularized.

1972 Federal Environmental Pesticide Control Act is established; Rural Development Act is passed; Clean Water Act is established.

1974 Safe Drinking Water Act is established.

1980 More farmers use no-till or low-till methods to curb erosion; biotechnology becomes viable for improving crop and livestock products.

1980 Railroad and trucking industries are deregulated.

1985 The 1985 Farm Bill is the first farm bill to contain a conservation title; it links conservation to eligibility for USDA program benefits.

1986 Antismoking campaigns and legislation begin to affect the tobacco industry.

1988 Scientists warn that global warming may affect the future viability of American farming; one of the worst droughts in the nation's history hits midwestern farmers.

1990s Information technology and precision techniques are increasingly used in agriculture; consolidation of rail lines reduces transportation options for rural residents.

1994 Natural Resources Conservation Service is created; farmers begin using satellite technology to track and plan their farming practices; the use of conservation tillage methods continues to rise.

1996 The 1996 Farm Bill makes significant changes and additions to the conservation title.

1996 Net farm income reaches a record $54.9 billion.

1997 The first weed and insect-resistant biotech crops (soybeans and cotton) become available commercially.

1998 Transportation Equity Act for the Twenty-first Century greatly increases highway spending.

1999 Price slump is caused by large commodity surpluses.

2000 USDA unveils organic standards and official organic seal; first DNA sequencing of a plant genome, the flowering mustard *Arabidopsis thaliana*.

2006 The USDA and Department of Energy host, for the first time in history, a conference to discuss the future of renewable energy; this coincides with President George W. Bush's Advanced Energy Initiative (AEI)—an aggressive plan to reduce U.S. dependence on foreign oil.

Adapted from the U.S. Department of Agriculture Education and Outreach Program, Agricultural Research Service (ARS) research timeline, ARS Headquarters, Washington, D.C. Also at: www.ars.usda.gov.

agroforestry   An intensive land management system that optimizes forestry and agricultural land uses. In this practice, trees or shrubs are deliberately combined with crops or livestock, allowing multiple uses to exist on a single area of land.

alternative farming   Farming methods that use techniques other than traditional plowing and cultivating; the emphasis is placed on more environmentally friendly practices.

aquaculture   The cultivation of aquatic (marine) organisms, such as fish, shellfish, algae, and other aquatic plants.

arable land   Land that can be used for growing food.

baler   A piece of farming equipment that collects cut hay and bundles it into bales; bales can be either circular or rectangular.

biodiversity   The existence of many different types of plant and animal species in an environment.

census   A count, or tally, of every person or item in a population, often including the collection of related demographic information.

combine   A harvesting machine that heads, threshes, and cleans grain while moving over a field.

commodity   An article of trade or commerce, especially an agricultural or mining product that can be processed and resold.

conservation   The protection, preservation, management, or restoration of wildlife and natural resources, such as forests, soil, and water.

Conservation Reserve Program   A program whose intent is to protect and conserve a specific resource.

conservationists   People who practice conservation.

contour plowing   A form of conservation in which a field is plowed, terraced, and planted to work with topography rather than against it, thereby reducing erosion.

crop rotation   Growing a series of different crops, one after the other, in the same field; this practice reduces the threat from pests and disease and helps the soil to stay fertile.

desertification   The process by which arable land becomes desert, usually from land mismanagement or climate change.

discing   A method of weed removal that uses a series of concave discs pulled by a tractor, which digs into the soil, lifting and turning over the weeds.

drought   A long period of abnormally low rainfall, especially one that adversely affects growing or living conditions.

Dust Bowl   Region of the United States that suffered from prolonged droughts and dust storms.

ecological niche   The positions within an ecosystem where an organism is best able to survive and thrive.

ecosystems   Relationships between organisms and their environment.

ecosystem health   The condition of the ecosystem and how well it provides for the organisms that live within it.

erosion   The action or process of wearing away the surface of the land, especially by the forces of wind, water, and ice.

evaporation   To convert into vapor. For example, when water evaporates, it is converted into water vapor.

evapotranspiration   Loss of water from the soil by evaporation and transpiration from the plants growing there.

fallow   Land left unplanted so it can recover its fertility.

famine   An extreme scarcity, or shortage, of food.

farmer's markets   Community gatherings and endeavors where those that have grown crops meet in a common location to sell their goods. They are popular in rural areas because the produce is very fresh.

farmer's year   The productive cycle for arable land. Planting usually begins in the spring, when the ground is not frozen. Fields are plowed, and seeds are sowed. Crops are cultivated during the summer growing season and usually harvested in the fall.

fertile   Producing or bearing in great quantities.

fertilizers Any of a large number of natural and synthetic materials, including manure and nitrogen, phosphorus, and potassium compounds, spread on or worked into the soil to increase its capacity to support plant growth.

forage Food for animals, especially obtained from browsing or grazing.

genetics A branch of biology that deals with the heredity and variation of organisms.

germinate The process of a seed sprouting.

germplasm The hereditary material of the germ cells; genes.

green energy production The production of energy using renewable resources instead of fossil fuels.

ground cover A planting of low plants that covers the ground in place of turf (grass).

harvest To gather in a crop.

herbal A substance that uses, or is made of, herbs.

herbicides Agents used to destroy or inhibit plant growth.

horticulture The science and art of growing fruits, vegetables, flowers, and ornamental plants.

humus A brown or black material composed of partially decomposed plant or animal matter and forming the organic portion of soil.

hydroponics The cultivation of plants without soil. These plants are grown in mediums such as water, sand, peat moss, and rock wool.

infestation To live in, or on, as a parasite.

infrastructure The underlying foundation or basic framework of a system; it includes the resources required for an activity (such as roads, processing plants, equipment, and markets).

land stewardship The concept of managing the land in order to allow for continued fertility and productivity for future generations.

leaching To dissolve by the action of a percolating liquid.

malnutrition A faulty nutrition due to the inadequate or unbalanced intake of nutrients, or their unsuccessful utilization.

manure   Livestock waste products (excrement) often mixed with straw and used to fertilize land.

native plants   Plants that originated in the area in which they are presently growing.

nonrenewable resource   A resource that either takes longer than one generation to replenish itself or cannot be replaced. Examples include soil, coal, and fossil fuels.

nutrient   Any of the mineral substances that are absorbed by the roots of plants and are necessary for the plants' growth.

organic farming   A method of farming that produces organic food. It differs from conventional farming in that chemicals are not used on the ground or crops.

overgrazing   When animals are allowed to graze in a pasture to the point of damaging the vegetative cover.

oxygenator   A medium that provides oxygen to something else.

perennial crops   Crops that emerge and grow each year without having to be replanted.

pesticides   Chemicals or natural agents used to kill pests, such as insects.

photosynthesis   A synthesis of chemical compounds with the aid of sunlight. It is the formation of carbohydrates from carbon dioxide and a source of hydrogen (water) in the chlorophyll-containing tissues of plants exposed to light.

public lands   Lands administered and cared for by the U.S. federal government for the benefit and use of all citizens. Examples include national parks, forests, and recreation areas.

purify   To make something clean, or to free it from undesirable elements.

quotas   Shares or proportions, assigned to each member of a group; fixed numbers or percentages.

renewable resource A resource that can be replenished in less than one generation. This type of resource can be replaced by natural ecological cycles or sound management practices.

shelter belts Tree windbreaks used in conservation practices.

soil conservation The protection of, and care for, soil resources in order to maintain soil fertility and prevent erosion and other types of damage.

Soil Conservation Service (SCS) A branch of the U.S. government whose mission is to provide for conservation of the nation's soil resources.

soil salinity control Measures used on soil to reduce salinity.

strip plowing A method of conservation farming.

subsidy A grant or gift of money. Concerning agriculture, it is money given from the government to assist farmers in their business.

symbiotic In a state of living or working together.

terracing A method of conservation farming that involves a series of horizontal ridges made in a hillside to increase cultivatable land, conserve moisture, and minimize erosion.

tillers Machines that prepare a field for planting and cultivation.

tilth The composition of soil in relation to its suitability for crop growth.

topsoil The surface of the soil, including the organic layer in which plants have most of their roots and which the farmer turns over in plowing.

transpiration The passage of watery vapor from a living body (such as a plant) through a membrane or pores.

watershed A region or area that is bounded peripherally by a divide and that drains ultimately into a particular watercourse or body of water.

FURTHER READING

PUBLICATIONS

Beck, Malcolm. *The Secret Life of Compost.* Metairie, La.: Acres U.S.A., 1997.

Bowman, Keith. *Agriculture.* Morristown, N.J.: Silver Burdett Press, 1985.

Chrisp, Peter. *The Farmer Through History.* New York: Thomson Learning, 1993.

Clemings, Russell. *Mirage: The False Promise of Desert Agriculture.* San Francisco: Sierra Club Books, 1996.

Ditchfield, Christin. *Soil.* New York: Children's Press, 2002.

Fite, Gilbert C. *The Farmers' Frontier: 1865–1900.* New York: Holt, Rinehart and Winston, 1966.

Floethe, Louise, and Richard Floethe. *Farming Around the World.* New York: Charles Scribner's Sons, 1970.

Halberstadt, April. *Plows and Planting Implements.* Osceola, Wis.: MBI Publishing Company, 1997.

Hays, Samuel P. *Conservation and the Gospel of Efficiency.* Pittsburgh, Pa.: University of Pittsburgh Press, 1959.

Horne, James E., and Maura McDermott. *The Next Green Revolution: Essential Steps to a Healthy, Sustainable Agriculture.* New York: Food Products Press, 2001.

Hudson, Norman. *Soil Conservation.* Ithaca, N.Y.: Cornell University Press, 1981.

Jackson, Wes. *New Roots for Agriculture.* Lincoln: University of Nebraska Press, 1980.

Myers, Norman. *A Wealth of Wild Species: Storehouse for Human Welfare.* Boulder, Colo.: Westview Press Inc., 1983.

Naar, Jon, and Alex J. Narr. *This Is Your Land: A Guide to North America's Endangered Ecosystems.* New York: HarperCollins, 1993.

Paddock, Joe, Nancy Paddock, and Carol Bly. *Soil and Survival: Land Stewardship and the Future of American Agriculture.* San Francisco: Sierra Club Books, 1986.

Pittman, Nancy P. *From the Land.* Washington, D.C.: Island Press, 1988.

Ponting, Clive. *A Green History of the World.* New York: Penguin Books, 1991.

Reay, P.J. *Aquaculture.* Baltimore, Md.: University Park Press, 1979.

Resh, Howard M. *Hydroponics: Questions and Answers for Successful Growing.* Santa Barbara, Calif.: Woodbridge Press, 1998.

Rifkin, Jeremy. *Biosphere Politics.* New York: Crown Publishers, 1991.

Roodman, David Malin. *The Natural Wealth of Nations: Harnessing the Market for the Environment.* New York: W.W. Norton & Company, 1998.

Schwab, Glenn O., Delmar D. Fangmeier, William J. Elliot, and Richard K. Frevert. *Soil and Water Conservation Engineering.* New York: John Wiley & Sons, 1993.

Sinnes, A. Cort. *All About Fertilizers, Soils and Water.* San Francisco: Ortho Books, 1979.

Sproule, Anna. *Food for the World.* New York: Facts on File, 1987.

Stein, Edith C. *The Environmental Sourcebook.* New York: Lyons and Burford, 1992.

Walters, Charles, and C.J. Fenzau. *Eco-Farm.* Metairie, La.: Acres U.S.A., 1996.

Wendel, C.H. *Encyclopedia of American Farm Implements and Antiques.* Iola, Wis.: Krause Publications, 1997.

WEB SITES

Agricultural Research Service

http://www.ars.usda.gov
Experiments, research, and new developments.

Agriculture in the Classroom

http://www.agclassroom.org/ut
Educational information for the Agriculture in the Classroom program.

American Coalition for Ethanol
http://www.ethanol.org
The production of ethanol as an alternative renewable energy resource.

ATTRA-National Sustainable Agriculture Information Service
http://www.attra.org
Conservation farming practices and sustainable agriculture.

Cooperative State Research, Education, and Extension Service
http://www.csrees.usda.gov
Research and current events.

Envirolink
http://www.envirolink.org
Ecosystem health and environmental issues.

Environmental Working Group
http://www.ewg.org
Pesticides and other environmental issues.

Missouri Corn Online
http://www.mocorn.org
Research, development, and the future of ethanol products.

National Agricultural Library
http://www.nal.usda.gov
Sustainable agriculture and alternative farming systems.

National Food and Energy Council
http://www.nfec.org
Alternative fuel sources.

National 4-H Headquarters
http://www.national4-hheadquarters.gov
How to become involved in community and personal projects.

Natural Resources Conservation Service
http://www.nrcs.usda.gov
Conservation practices, research, and local applications.

PBS: Earth on the Edge
http://www.pbs.org
All aspects of ecosystems and environmental conservation.

Space Agriculture in the Classroom
http://www.spaceag.org
The combined Web site of NASA, USDA, and the University of Florida. Space studies involving agriculture.

Union of Concerned Scientists
http://www.ucsusa.org
Biotechnology, food, and the environment.

United States Department of Agriculture
http://www.usda.gov
Agricultural practices, projects, news, research, and educational information.

United States Department of the Interior, Bureau of Land Management
http://www.blm.gov
Grazing and rangeland management as well as identification and eradication of noxious weeds.

ORGANIZATIONS

4-H Clubs

4-H Youth Development Program

National 4-H Headquarters

Cooperative State Research, Education, and Extension Service

U.S. Department of Agriculture

1400 Independence Ave., S.W., Stop 2225

Washington, DC 20250-2225

(202) 720-2908

http://www.national4-hheadquarters.gov

Future Farmers of America

National FFA Center

P.O. Box 68960, 6060 FFA Drive

Indianapolis, IN 46268-0960

(317) 802-6060

http://www.ffa.org/

National Food and Energy Council

PO Box 309

2333 Rombach Ave.

Wilmington, OH 45177

(937) 383-0001

http://www.nfec.org/

JULIE KERR CASPER holds B.S., M.S., and Ph.D. degrees in earth science with an emphasis on natural resource conservation. She has worked for the United States Bureau of Land Management (BLM) for nearly 30 years and is primarily focused on practical issues concerning the promotion of a healthier, better-managed environment for both the short- and long-term. She has also had extensive experience teaching middle school and high school students over the past 20 years. She has taught classes, instructed workshops, given presentations, and led field trips and science application exercises. She is also the author of several award-winning novels, articles, and stories.